# SYLVESTER STALLONE

## A Rocky Life

# About the Author

Frank Sanello has written biographies on Tom Cruise, Steven Spielberg, Sharon Stone, Jimmy Stewart, Will Smith and the current bestseller, *Eddie Murphy: The Life and Times of a Comic on the Edge*.

As a journalist for the past 25 years, Sanello has written for the *Washington Post*, the *Chicago Tribune*, the *New York Times* Syndicate, *People*, *Cosmo* and *Penthouse* magazines. He was also the film critic for the Los Angeles *Daily News* and a business reporter for United Press International.

A native of Joliet, Illinois, Sanello graduated from the University of Chicago with honours and earned a Master's Degree from UCLA's film school. A purple belt in Tae Kwon Do, Sanello volunteers as a martial arts instructor at AIDS Project Los Angeles.

His upcoming biography, *Will Smith: Safe for Stardom*, examines the joys and frustrations of being the number one box-office star in Hollywood – and a black man in a largely white industry.

A writer with wide-ranging interests, Sanello is currently working on a popular history, tentatively titled, *China's Opium Wars: Substance Abuse as Foreign Policy*, which will apply modern theories of drug addiction to nineteenth-century politics.

The author lives in West Hollywood, California, with two dogs and three cats.

# STALLONE
## A Rocky Life

*Frank Sanello*

MAINSTREAM
PUBLISHING

EDINBURGH AND LONDON

For the survivors:
Marshmallow, Wendy, Cesare, Lucrezia and Catullus

First published in Great Britain in 1998 by
MAINSTREAM PUBLISHING COMPANY (EDINBURGH) LTD
7 Albany Street
Edinburgh EH1 3UG

ISBN 1 84018 113 3

A catalogue record for this book is available from the British Library

Typeset in Caslon
Printed and bound in Finland by WSOY Book Printing Division

# Contents

| | | |
|---|---|---|
| | Introduction | 7 |
| 1 | Hellish Kitchen | 13 |
| 2 | Back in the Not So Good Old US of A | 38 |
| 3 | Lord of Flatbush | 55 |
| 4 | Rocking the Boat | 61 |
| 5 | Post-Euphoria Depression | 80 |
| 6 | F.I.S.T.-icuffs | 93 |
| 7 | Roman Numerology | 104 |
| 8 | The Ring Cycle Continues | 116 |
| 9 | A Very Cold Warrior | 123 |
| 10 | Italian Stallions | 130 |
| 11 | The Sad Case of Seargeoh Stallone | 133 |
| 12 | Bodycounts and Box-office | 145 |
| 13 | Cold War Sizzles on Screen | 150 |
| 14 | Rambo Tries Arm Wrestling | 159 |
| 15 | Stallion in Drawing-Room = Bull in China Shop | 165 |
| 16 | Method Eating | 174 |
| 17 | A Rocky Love Life | 184 |

# Introduction

# Fear and Self-loathing on the Riviera

Even the paparazzi stopped clicking for a second during the press conference at the Cannes Film Festival in May 1997. There was Sylvester Stallone, a superstar whose films over the past quarter century had grossed $4 billion, publicly apologising for the last ten years of his career. Not since Medieval *flagellantes* beat themselves up in public has a *mea culpa* taken such a sackcloth and grosses approach. Basically, the superstar repudiated the essence of his professional life and success, action films.

Cannes is designed for self-congratulatory back-slapping, not self-denouncing back-stabbing, at least not stabbing yourself. There's a famous joke that you can tell who your real friends are in Hollywood. They're the ones who stab you in the *front*. In Stallone's case, he may have agreed with Pogo's philosophy of warfare: 'We have met the enemy, and they are us!'

Indeed, many critics and even fans felt that for the previous decade, if not longer, Stallone had been his own worst enemy – at least when it came to picking movie projects. In his personal life, he also seemed to be shooting himself in the foot – or more precisely, the heart – as he flitted from one failed liaison to another until finally settling down with his girlfriend of nine years after she got pregnant.

'I despise the last ten years,' he said at a press conference outside Cannes' Hotel du Cap on the boardwalk known as La Croisette overlooking the French Riviera. Although he had made his name and fortune killing more people on screen than a mass murderer in real life, Stallone regretted the violence he had perpetuated and glorified in his films. 'Well, I do apologise [about] random, senseless violence. Because in many films, about halfway through, there was no real challenge, I think I would lose focus and then, when the smoke would clear a year later, I would see the end result and I would have nothing but absolute contempt! I wasn't trying to make it really special.' He was trying to make a buck, he admitted, which he had already more than enough of. 'I accepted the money and everything and it became a job. I think when art becomes a job it is no longer art.'

Being a superstar is a dirty job, but somebody has to do it, Burt Reynolds, another star down on his box-office, once joked. Stallone, however, was being too hard on himself when he added, 'Even though I'm known, when you're talking about serious film-making, I would never be considered.' If only he had had a crystal ball at Cannes, because a year later the American Film Institute not only considered, but included his work in its Top 100 list of the greatest American films ever made. Listed at number 78, ahead of films by acknowledged masters like Martin Scorsese (*Goodfellas*, number 94) and even Charlie Chaplin (*Modern Times*, number 81), was a little sleeper Stallone had not only starred in but written, *Rocky*. (Another survey at the time indicated he was the fifth most successful screenwriter of the past decade. Films which he wrote had earned more than half a billion dollars.)

But that official recognition was a year away. Meanwhile, Stallone took his *flagellante* act on the road as he promoted his new, low-budget, low-octane character drama, *Cop Land*, across Europe after Cannes. The self-lashing and trashing continued. 'I've had success few people can dream of, but for the past 11 years I have led a shallow and egotistical life. My eyes have been opened, and I'm turning over a new leaf,' he said at the opening in Rome of Planet Hollywood, part of his enormously successful restaurant chain. Back home in Miami, he said, 'I'd like to be able to remember the movie longer than the time it takes to get to my car.' On another occasion, however, he said he would rather forget most of his movies.

As Stallone's self-denunciations made headlines across Europe, a development in America barely made the gossip columns. While Stallone was in Cannes with Harvey Weinstein, whose Miramax Films had produced *Cop Land* and given Stallone a new chance at respectability, the company's co-chairman and Harvey's brother, Bob Weinstein, was hanging out in a Los Angeles courtroom, where a bankruptcy proceeding was underway. Up for grabs – sequel rights to the film library of Carolco Pictures.

Miramax, called the Tiffany's of independents, even though it's owned by Disney, only wanted the cream of Carolco's crap, however. For the firesale price of $500,000, the savvy Weinstein *frère* bought the rights to *Rambo*, whose three films had grossed more than one billion dollars worldwide. While Stallone was at Cannes apologising for his violent past on screen, including John Rambo, Weinstein was planning a Faustian bargain with which he hoped to tempt the repentant sinner back to the cinema of high explosives and low expectations.

The *Rambo* coup occurred only a few days after the star's press conference at Cannes, but it didn't get much press attention since so many movies had Stallone's name tenuously attached. One production executive joked, 'I heard he just signed for *Christ II.*'

In 1997 at Cannes, Stallone had said action movies 'are dead and buried now. I want to make films that stick in the memory a little longer.' A year later, also at Cannes, Dimension Films, a Miramax subsidiary, was hustling distribution rights to *Rambo IV*. The project needed a big hustle, since it had a budget of $75 million. What made the announcement really newsworthy, however, was that Sylvester Stallone had agreed to re-arm himself for the role.

What had lured Stallone away from the art house back to the fun house of popcorn flicks? It couldn't have been money. He already had a $60 million, three-picture deal at Universal, although none of those films had gotten anywhere near a soundstage.

An unnamed friend of the actor insisted Stallone hadn't gone back to the same well for his usual $20 million per pic fee. The colleague said the fourth *Rambo* would present a kinder, gentler psychopath, 'more introspective and thoughtful, with character development'. The story would have the hero thwarting an Oklahoma City-like bomb attack on a government building.

Miramax, playing Mephistopheles to Stallone's Faust, offered the cinematic equivalent of Helen of Troy. The Weinsteins would put its Oscar-winning stable of writers and directors at Rambo's disposal. The list included everyone from the Merchant-Ivory team to the creators of *The English Patient* and *The Wings of the Dove*. John Rambo, meet your new screenwriter, the ghost of Henry James!

In those terms, the pact seemed less Faustian and more like just plain smart. But this spin on Stallone's decision to strap on the bandolero again was undercut by yet another announcement in the trades. Miramax was trying to sign up the original producers of *Rambo*, *First Blood*'s Andrew Vajna and Mario Kassar. The producers were also the founders of Carolco, whose bankruptcy proceedings the Weinsteins had turned into a flea market.

At Cannes, Stallone had sought absolution by offering up *Cop Land* as penance. Instead of $20 million, he had accepted 50 grand to play a fat cop. In a further act of self-mutilation, he stopped working out and gained 40 pounds to get in character.

With *Rambo*'s *auteurs* rather than James Ivory and Ismail Merchant back on board, and Stallone packing 18-inch guns (that's bodybuilder-speak for biceps, not weapons), what will Stallone say when he returns to Cannes, probably in the year 2000, with a fresh print of *Rambo IV* and a stale reworking of the vigilante who looks like a Michelangelo model?

The devil made him do it?

Or maybe he will blame Bob and Harvey, pulling a fast one, substituting Vajna and Kassar for James (Henry) and James (Ivory).

See you on La Croisette at the millennium.

* * *

Why the superstar felt compelled to apologise, then renege on his promise to do more worthy projects by returning to a sure thing like *Rambo*, is puzzling, but not entirely inexplicable. A self-admitted sense of inadequacy, fostered by those closest to him in childhood, helps explain the revolving *volte-faces* that define the life of Sylvester Enzio Stallone.

# Chapter One

# Hellish Kitchen

'You weren't born with much of a brain, so you'd better develop your body.' – *Frank Stallone Sr to his son, Sylvester*

Burgess Meredith says those words to Sylvester Stallone in the first *Rocky* film. But Stallone, who also wrote the script, later revealed he was actually quoting his real-life father, a failed nightclub singer who became a successful hairdresser.

To say Stallone was an abused child grossly understates a grotesque upbringing – like saying Christina Crawford didn't get along with her mother Joan.

The future superstar's traumatic childhood literally began at birth with a surgical trauma. The Stallones were broke. Mom Jackie's aspirations as a chorus girl had detoured into selling cigarettes from a tray at nightclubs. Dad was still struggling to get his hair salon off the ground. They lived on Ninth Avenue in the blighted neighbourhood known as Hell's Kitchen on New York's Lower East Side.

The family was too poor to afford a private physician, and when Mrs Stallone went into labour, she ended up in the charity ward of a public hospital. Prophetically, the hospital was across the street from the Actors Studio, the artistic birthplace of Marlon Brando, Marilyn Monroe and Dustin Hoffman.

Even the trip there involved a fight between mom and dad. Hard up for cash, Jacqueline Stallone refused to take a taxi to the hospital even after her waters broke. She also wanted to eat lunch before taking the bus.

The doctor on duty was an intern, and he didn't know what he was doing. Born on 6 July 1946, the future heavyweight weighed 13 pounds at birth, and it was a difficult delivery. The unsupervised intern clamped forceps on to the baby's face and pulled . . . hard. The surgical instrument severed a facial nerve, which created Stallone's trademark drooping eyelid and lips and also a speech impediment which over the years has largely disappeared thanks to the services of a therapist. Stallone attributes his *basso profundo* to this natal injury as well. Or in his elegant phrase, 'I have the voice of a Mafia pallbearer.'

While mom stinted on taxi fare, Stallone later blamed his father for the taxi's destination – the charity ward – and by implication, the obstetrical injury that left him permanently scarred. 'My father wouldn't spend the money for a proper hospital, so I was delivered by interns instead of doctors,' he said.

A fight at the hospital over the baby's name was averted only because Jacqueline was sedated after the difficult delivery. When it came time to fill out the birth certificate, she was out cold. Jacqueline had planned to name her son after her favourite actor, Tyrone Power. Tyrone Stallone – a rhyming name would have made him the butt of children's jokes and a laughable marquee moniker for an aspiring actor. The name his father chose, however, was almost as bad, Sylvester Enzio, his paternal grandfather's name. 'Sylvester' would have to endure a childhood and adolescence of cracks about 'Sylvester the Cat' and 'Tweety Pie'. Sylvester, however, turned out to be too much of a mouthful even for a traditional Sicilian like Frank, Sr, and the baby ended up being called 'Binky'.

In later years, critics would complain about his lack of facial expressiveness and monotone voice. What they were really criticising however, was a birth defect – partial facial paralysis! Fans, especially female ones, would eventually consider the droopy eye and pouty lips sexy. Stallone, on the other hand, felt deformed and would compensate for the imperfection above his neck by creating perfection below – the best bod in Hollywood. Over a lifetime of making lemonade out of lemons, Stallone transformed his 'deformity', a lopsided face and vocal limitations, into a movie franchise that has grossed $4 billion.

Or as he described the 'up side' of the surgical assault: 'Forceps damage severed the nerve above my jaw. It caused this deep voice and this slant on my mouth, which gives me a snarling look. It comes in handy for *Rambo*, but it's a disadvantage if you want to put on a friendly face to strangers.'

One man's grotesque birth defect is another man's window of opportunity, motivation to overachieve and overcompensate. 'When you have an abnormality, you become a focal point for scorn and ridicule. And that may be one of the reasons I apply myself so hard. People who have had tremendous setbacks in their lives are driven with a maniacal intensity that is incomprehensible to someone who's had a normal life,' the actor said.

Sylvester Stallone did not have a normal life. The gross encounter with the surgical pliers was just the beginning of a hellish childhood that would have turned a less resilient personality into a criminal or a disturbed adult at the very least.

Both his parents were career-obsessed, as their son would eventually become himself. His mother, he said, was 'talented and outgoing. She had opportunities to get ahead, but when she became pregnant with me, she had to adhere to responsibilities. I don't know if she blamed me, but she certainly uses it [his birth] as a turning point. I guess I slowed her down.'

Mom's 'opportunities' mostly revolved around dancing as one of the 'Long Stemmed Roses' at the Billy Rose Diamond Horseshoe nightclub in New York until, in her son's words, 'she ate too much Wonderbread', i.e., got fat, and the term 'long-stemmed' no longer applied. But while Jacqueline continued to tap away and sell cigarettes in clubs that didn't value her dancing talent, she was too busy to care for her son.

'I was a sickly, hyperactive child. My mother didn't have the time or inclination needed to care for me properly,' he said. 'Love was not that forthcoming. My parents had their difficulties, so there wasn't any time for me or my younger brother, Frank. It wasn't a tranquil household. There was great chaos.' Also, great poverty. Stallone was of course exaggerating but not fabricating his early years' deprivation when he said, 'Poor? When you suck a radiator for heat, *that* is poor.'

Actually, most of the time, the Stallones' cold-water flat *was* fairly tranquil because it was empty. From the age of two to five, Stallone and Frank Jr who was born in 1950, were boarded weekdays with a foster mother in Queens. The kids spent weekends with their parents. For reasons never explained, the foster mother rarely spoke to either child. During these crucial formative years, Stallone grew up in a non-verbal fantasy world. Psychologists might say that his terse screenplays (*Rambo* has only 136 lines of dialogue) and their outlandish plots reflected both aspects of his emotionally deprived, silent childhood.

But the abuse wasn't only emotional, and it didn't just involve deprivation. While Jackie's parenting consisted of benign neglect, Frank Sr took a more hands-on approach to child-rearing when the Stallone boys returned home on weekends from silent fostercare.

'His idea of discipline was very physical,' Stallone said about a father who obviously had never read Dr Spock. 'There were times I was in mortal fear of him.

'My father was an extraordinarily exacting man, and if what you did wasn't a photocopy of the way he did it then you had no abilities and had to be chastised and corrected. And quite often the correction was, you know, shocking. He made me feel extraordinarily inept.'

His father alternated between emotional and physical assaults. Sylvester recapped on his dad's litany of reproach: 'Why can't you be smarter? Why can't you be stronger?'

A man who would eventually develop 18-inch arms, a 50-inch chest and a personal fortune of $200 million years later still smarted at the recollection of this parental criticism. 'I didn't have one virtue. He never said he was proud of me. He was very judgemental, and I was always being judged guilty. I grew up with a pretty profound complex of inadequacy.' His father's favourite description of his son's brain was 'dormant'.

Indeed, after *Rocky* became the number one film of 1976 and collected a trophy case full of Oscars, the elder Stallone's only comment was, 'The fight scenes could have been better.' Sylvester found himself making excuses as an adult for his father's behaviour when he was a child. 'I understand none of this was hatred. It's just his nature to be extremely critical.'

And extremely physical. 'I was swatted a few times with great power. I was sent flying, a heat-seeking missile across the room. I would get difficult spankings.'

Whether it's denial or acceptance, Stallone downplays the abuse by comparing it to worse scenarios which he never experienced. 'The 'abused' label is not as valid . . . because today when we think of abused children, we think of people with acid burns, whipped, tortured with cigarette butts on the heels of their feet. It was never that. It was just a very strong upbringing in the sense that if you did something wrong, the hammer fell.'

At other times, he didn't minimise the severity of the abuse, describing the Stallone apartment as 'a house of nightmares, a carnival of horrors. I wanted to be anybody but me.'

To this day, the sound of whistling causes something akin to post-traumatic stress syndrome, the kind of flashback that causes Vietnam vets to duck for cover when a car backfires. A visitor to the set of one of his films was warned, 'Whatever you do, don't whistle around Sly.' Although the reporter hadn't really planned to whistle a happy tune while chatting up the superstar, he was intrigued by the order and wanted to know why. The production assistant explained, 'His father used to whistle just before he'd beat the living shit out of him.'

Also in flashback mode, Stallone finds it painful to discuss these years of abuse. In interview after interview over more than a quarter century, he typically offers a glimpse of his traumatic upbringing, then backs off, leaving the luckless reporter with a dangling anecdote. Once, perhaps as a purgative, his wife urged him in front of a reporter to expand on his comment, 'Tough, extremely tough, my father.'

'You haven't said yet just how tough,' his then wife Sasha prompted him. Stallone's terse but powerful metaphor for the physical abuse was, 'Let's just say he communicated with, uh, *volatile* sign language.'

Dad ruled with an iron fist and at times their physical dialogue became positively garrulous. 'That's the way he communicated – the old back-hand-across-the-teeth syndrome. The Mafia had the Black Hand; my father had the back hand.'

His father's toughness was illustrated with a preposterous anecdote that is probably, nonetheless, true. Stallone said: 'He's more like Stanley Kowalski. I've seen him eat a raw sparrow.' Unlike other celebrities' parents who cash in on their offspring's fame, the elder Stallone will probably never publish a cookbook like *Poultry Tartare – Frank Stallone's Favourite Recipes*.

On another occasion, Stallone elaborated on his father's taste for game *tartare*. It would be natural to think the younger Stallone was describing his father's culinary taste with tongue planted firmly in cheek, but immediately after describing dad's amusing yen for raw meat, he mentioned other behaviour by his father which might be called 'fist in face' rather than tongue in cheek.

'My father is very primitive. I've seen him knock out a horse. Split himself open and stitch himself up. Shoot a rabbit and right on the spot, split it in half and eat its entrails, steaming.'

Dad's brutish ways with food and family came from a failure to communicate, Stallone said years later in a forgiving mood, 'I think my father never really learned to communicate in the way which he always wishes he could have, which is with the written word. So I think that his calling card on the planet is how physically aggressive he can be.

'I was terrified. I always longed for the Norman Rockwellian father. I never recall a day when he taught me to play baseball, taught me to play basketball. I was always being judged: guilty, not guilty, guilty. Pay the price.'

When the verdict came down 'guilty', the price was often physical punishment. Asked point blank by a reporter from *Details* magazine in 1994, 'Did your father ever beat you?' Stallone finally stopped hedging and said after some embarrassed hesitation, 'Well . . . there were times when, you might say, I was unconscious. Literally. When I was 12 or 13, he sent me to the store to get some bread, and I met some friends. He came out and found me there and blasted me out. Sprawled.'

While his older brother remains reticent about their early years, his brother Frank Jr is more upfront. Frank said in a cover story in *Newsweek* in 1977, 'I hate my family, except my brother. Our parents were very inconsistent with us, and Sly went through much undue physical and emotional abuse from them. We grew up in not a happy household. It was every man for himself. It's not that we grew up as urchins. It was just unhappy. But my brother and I were always close. We fought sometimes but we loved each other. To some extent, he has been a father figure for me.'

The potential for hateful sibling rivalry was great but never occurred. Unlike his older brother, who had facial flaws and a speech impediment, Frank was a beautiful child who had inherited his father's singing talent without his father's crippling shyness. Mom and dad lavishly praised the baby of the family and encouraged him with expensive music lessons that they couldn't afford. This clear preference, however, never poisoned the Stallone boys' relationship.

Indeed, the mutal affection continues to this day, something that can't be said about many of Stallone's other relationships, personal or professional. Throughout the years, Sylvester has gone out of his way to help his brother's acting and recording career, going so far as to do a cameo in a no-budget film in which his brother starred, in order to secure financing.

The fight scenes at home were perhaps more violent if not as well choreographed as *Rocky*'s, but real hatred made up for a bad 'script'. Stallone described his parents' battles as a war between the 'black and the red ants'.

His recollections of their romantic relationship changed and contradicted each other over the years. He told one interviewer that passion did not bind his parents but failed to explain why they got together in the first place. 'My mother and my father were not very amorous. Paraphrasing her, one night he tripped on a banana peel, fell into bed, and she was impregnated. It was not planned.'

On another occasion, his parents seem to be red-blooded cast members in A *Streetcar Named Desire*, two very different personalities joined by that great unifier, animal lust. 'There's a real animalistic, Stanley Kowalski kind of Neanderthal charm about my father, and I mean that in a positive way. [Jacqueline Stallone] liked to be dominated, and then she resented it.'

The romance flourished until opposites began to repel, not attract. 'In the beginning,' his parents' love was 'very, very intense, but my mother was extremely bull-headed. She really had an extremely artistic bent. She comes from great intelligence. Together you had a combination of the physical and the mental, so there was a real battle there in a sense.' Frank was doing a brutish Stanley; Jackie a cerebral Stella.

While both were inordinately ambitious, career obsession followed by career failure seemed to be their only common bond. Born in Sicily, where his son claims he was a shepherd, Frank Sr came to America as a child with ambitions in showbiz, not animal husbandry. Possessing a mellifluous singing voice, the immigrant dreamt of becoming a lounge singer like his idol, Perry Como.

Unlike his extroverted offspring, however, dad was shy everywhere except in the home boxing ring. 'My father was flipping out. His frustration came because he wanted to be an entertainer – he had a magnificent singing voice – and could have been a good entertainer in the Perry Como mould, but he had paralysing stage fright. So he would sing in burlesque houses behind the curtain. I guess I inherited the performing needs from both of them.'

Although both parents wanted to be stars, his mother's background was dramatically different from her husband's. Born Jacqueline Labofish, hers was a story of downward mobility, from a comfortable upper-class home to Hell's Kitchen and a cigarette tray as workplace.

While her husband's forebears were tending sheep in the hard-scrabble hills of Sicily, Jacqueline's father was presiding over District Court in the nation's capital. Legend or fact has it that like his future grandson, Judge Labofish was obsessed with bodybuilding and once roomed with Charles Atlas, the original dweeb turned muscle guru.

Although he liked to brag about his impoverished roots, Sylvester also loved to brag about his mother's side of the family, which didn't tend sheep. 'My grandfather was the highest-ranking circuit judge in Washington, DC, and also a 33rd-degree Mason. *His* father had patented a typewriter ribbon and written a definitive book on patent law. So one side of the family was quite erudite,' Stallone said with pride.

After the birth of a second child in 1950, the cold-water flat became too overcrowded even though the kids were in Queens five days a week. Fortunately, Frank Sr's salon began to prosper, and when Sylvester was four, the family fled Hell's Kitchen for the upper-class Washington suburb of Silver Springs, Maryland.

The family had saved money for the move to Maryland by scrimping on essentials, with disastrous effects on their son's health. During these years of artificial famine, Sylvester suffered from rickets, a disease more common to the Third World, and caused by a poor diet lacking in Vitamin D. One of the symptoms of rickets is restlessness, something that afflicts Stallone to this day. He remembered being so hyperactive that his mother put a lid on the crib after he kept wandering out of the apartment. At three, he climbed down the fire escape and a cop who found Sylvester toddling down the mean streets of Hell's Kitchen brought him home. At five, he tricycled so far from home he got lost and had to break open a fire-alarm box; and got a ride back in a firetruck.

As an adult, Stallone would give his life-long restlessness a clinical label, Attention Deficit Disorder. The highest-paid superstar at the time, Stallone found himself apologising to a reporter visiting the set. As he puttered around his Winnebago between takes, he said on the set of his 1995 film *Assassins*, 'Don't mind my flipping around here, but I suffer from a malady called 'attention span deficit', and I just *have* to move around.'

Although he tends to mythologise his impoverished upbringing, by the time he entered school, Sylvester Stallone's family was affluent. His father eventually owned a chain of salons, J. Frank's Hair Stylists. Frank Sr soon became rich enough to indulge the passion of his ancestors and bought a string of polo ponies. The former Sicilian shepherd became a landed 'aristocrat' and adept at the sport of kings, polo. Unfortunately, he found other uses for his riding crop besides motivating lazy ponies. According to the reputable magazine *Sports Illustrated*, 'Frank [Sr] used his riding crop on young Sly' too.

As a youth, Stallone tried to join in his father's passion, but dad humiliated instead of encouraging him. Once, after some *faux pas*, Frank yanked his son off his horse in the middle of a match. The younger Stallone abandoned the sport, but picked it up again years later.

Still seeking his father's approval as an adult and a major movie star, Stallone approached the sport again – but this time with the bankroll of a multi-millionaire. He didn't have any interest in the sport of kings, but he wanted to royally impress dad, who adamantly refused to be impressed.

Stallone set up a match on the number one polo field in America in Palm Beach, Florida, flying in the top-ranked players in the world at his own expense. In a rare moment of self-revelation, the elder Stallone confessed to his son that it had long been a dream of his to play at the world-famous Palm Beach venue.

The fantasy became reality when father and son joined these top professionals, but on opposing teams. At one point during the match, the son was hurled to the ground after another horse rammed its head into his horse. When Sylvester looked up from the dirt, he saw that it was his father who had hit him.

\* \* \*

A reporter from *US* magazine once asked Stallone if he had embellished his modest background. The star conceded that he had – up to a point. 'It *is* true. I mean, everyone likes to embellish their image, but the record shows I was born in Hell's Kitchen in New York, 50th and Tenth Avenue. My father was trying to make his way, my mother was working in a nightclub.

My father used to have to walk down the centre of the street at night, 'cause if you walked on the sidewalks you might just disappear from the face of the earth.' But then Stallone admitted this wasn't the entire story of his childhood. 'But eventually they pulled themselves out of that situation. By the time I was ten, eleven, they were doing quite well.'

Very well, indeed. Silver Springs is a leafy suburb more rural than suburban, with backyards that resemble parks. One biographer called the Stallone home a 'farm'. But the enhanced surroundings did not enhance Sylvester's attitude or behaviour. He remained, in his own words, a 'difficult child' and began to act up. At four, he claims he decided 'all the cars on the block should be painted red, and I proceeded to do that'. When he saw a horsefly on the hood of his father's car, he swatted it with a brick, hitting the car repeatedly.

It's impossible to overdramatise his self-loathing and negative body image at this time. 'I was not an attractive child. I was sickly and I even had rickets. I was scrawny, my mouth went to one side. I was like a poster boy for a nightmare. In a contest between me and a bulldog, you'd say the bulldog's better. My personality was abhorrent to the other children, so I enjoyed my own company and did a lot of fantasising.'

His peers contributed to his sense of inadequacy. 'Sylvester Puddytat' and 'Sylvester Tweetybird' were the kinder epithets hurled at him. More cruelly, kids focused on his facial paralysis and called him 'Slant Mouth' and 'Mr Potato Head'. Years later, he conceded the comparison to the famous child's toy might have been cruel, but it was also accurate. 'I *was* like Mr Potato Head, with all the parts in the wrong place.' Stallone ignored these taunts because he was ashamed to argue and expose his speech impediment as well. But when the kids called him a 'wop', he discovered his fists 'spoke' more eloquently than his slurred speech.

The original aversion turned to aggression. By his own account, he averaged one fight a month. Sensitised by abuse at home and school, he found any insult, no matter how minor, would set him off. 'Now, when I reflect on it, I realise it was just a burst of creative energy.' Other 'creative outbursts' included taping 'kick me' signs on his tormentors' backs and putting thumbtacks on their seats.

His rich fantasy life provided some escape until he made the mistake of sharing it with a classmate he mistook for a friend and confidant. In 1949, the first *Superboy* comic book came out, and the muscular kid with superhuman strength became the rickety, scrawny youngster's, well, superhero. Stallone put together a Superboy costume – blue leotard, red gymshorts, a sweatshirt with a giant 'S' drawn on it, and a barber's cape borrowed from his father's salon. He wore it under his regular clothes and told a friend about his secret identity. The 'friend' blabbed to the teacher, who made Stallone strip in front of the class and show off his costume. Stallone was humiliated and withdrew further into his fantasy world of a skinny kid with subterranean muscles. His adult life and career saw him living out the fantasy by developing a physique of near bodybuilder proportions.

At 11, he decided that like his superhero, he could fly – and jumped off the second floor of his Maryland home using an umbrella as an ineffectual 'parachute'. The youth broke his collarbone. He would have been killed if his father hadn't been mixing cement for a backyard barbecue pit. The trough provided a rough cushion for his landing. When his mother came running out of the house after hearing the splash, her husband's only response to the injured child was, 'This boy will never become President. You've given birth to an idiot.'

Finally, Jacqueline took her troubled son to a psychotherapist. Years later, his mother claimed the shrink suggested her son should be institutionalised. Stallone had a different recollection. He quoted the therapist as saying, 'The kid's fine – do something about the parents!'

Failing psychotherapy, as he had so many academic subjects, Stallone was sent by his parents on a religious retreat. In an eerie early variation on G. Gordon Liddy's preoccupation with pain and fire, Stallone was told by a priest to place his hand over a lit candle as an example of the fiery damnation that awaited him if he didn't change his delinquent ways. For a kid used to riding-crop whippings and broken collarbones, what was a little second-degree burn? 'Place your hand over the flame, and it will wither,' the priest ordered him. Stallone obliged, and left his hand there until even the priest's sadism rebelled and he ripped the youth's hand away.

The same year he fell off the roof, his parents finally admitted what they had known for years – they had fallen out of love – and divorced in 1957. The split was apparently amicable, since the parents agreed to joint custody, but it was a bizarre variation on the usual division of parental responsibility. The kids would spend one year with dad, then the next year with mom.

Sylvester hated this division of the spoils. As eccentric as Jacqueline was, he was traumatised when she left him with her ex-husband the first time. 'I hung on to her leg. I was in convulsions,' he said. The yearly trade off caused other problems. Already anti-social, unlike his gregarious sibling who made friends easily, Stallone found himself injected into a new atmosphere every year – with a whole new set of friends to make, or more likely, a whole new set of tormentors to fight.

Jacqueline, however, soon made a new life – and found a new love – for herself in Philadelphia, where she moved after the divorce. Her new husband, Tony Filiti, was even more affluent than her salon-owning ex. Filiti was Philly's pizza king, the owner of a factory that produced the frozen pies. Jacqueline later claimed Filiti was not her first suitor, but he *was* the first who wasn't scared off by her incorrigible elder son.

Unlike Frank, her new husband encouraged his wife's career outside the home, although by now she had wisely given up showbiz aspirations and decided to become an entrepreneur. *Sports Illustrated* inaccurately reported that the new Mrs Filiti's 'main exercise was social climbing'. Actually, her main exercise *was* exercise.

Maybe she too noticed, in her son's words, too much indulgence in 'Wonderbread'. So Jacqueline decided to open a gym for women, a unique concept in the '50s, when Marilyn Monroes, not future Kate Mosses, were the ideal feminine mystique/physique.

Worried that her son was headed for juvenile hall or worse, Mrs Filiti dragged him to her gym in which he was profoundly disinterested. That was until he saw the film *Hercules* in 1959. The star, former Mr Universe Steve Reeves, became an even more obsessive fantasy figure for him than the merely muscled Superboy. While other future actors would consider Brando's Method a seminal influence, Stallone found his inspiration in the craft of Steve Reeves. Or more specifically, in the crafted body of the handsome hulk.

'The first time I saw *On the Waterfront*, I fell asleep. But I practically tore the seats out of the theatre when I saw my first Steve Reeves picture,' Stallone said. 'The day I saw Steve Reeves is the day my life changed. It was like seeing the Messiah. I said, "This is what I want to be." I, of course, went overboard. There wasn't a piece of furniture in the house I wasn't lifting.' While Brando tended to mumble just as he did, Reeves *flexed*, something the newly minted bodybuilder found himself doing in front of the mirror a lot, as pictures from this period document.

Although earlier beefcake epics like Kirk Douglas's *The Vikings* and Burt Lancaster's *The Crimson Pirate* had fascinated Stallone, those stars looked more like gymnasts than gymrats. Reeves had the body of a cartoon superhero, except he was real – or as real as any two-dimensional movie image could be. The Reeves canon that followed the original *Hercules* had Sylvester living inside movie theatres for multiple screenings of *Hercules Unchained, Goliath and the Barbarians* and *The Thief of Baghdad*.

He could never fly like Superboy. In fact, acting out that fantasy almost killed him. But Stallone could approximate his Steve Reeves's fantasy. And all he had to do was go to work with mom! But the gym wasn't enough of a challenge. He dragged home auto parts from junkyards and used them as *ersatz* weights. Cinderblocks lashed to the ends of a broomstick served as unwieldy barbells.

Sylvester went from 'Mr Couch Potato Head' to a 13-year-old with 16-inch biceps. His mother was relieved that instead of bombing cars with bricks, he hit the weights even more aggressively. After years of absence caused by work and divorce, she saw more of him at the gym than she had ever seen in the cold-water flat on Ninth Avenue. But the improvement in his outer appearance couldn't hide an inner self-loathing that no striated pecs or vascular biceps could make go away. His father's comment, later repeated verbatim in the first *Rocky* film, didn't help his self-esteem either. As Sylvester's body blossomed on the bench press, his father punctured his 'pumpitude' with the now famous phrase: 'You weren't born with much of a brain, so you better develop your body.'

Less successfully, the insecure youth tried to develop both and embarked on an intellectual self-improvement regime almost as industrious as the gym workout. He decided to learn one new word every day from a dictionary he bought. To this day, Stallone's vocabulary in interviews is peppered with arcane words that have interviewers commenting with surprise how articulate the star is, especially compared to his monosyllabic film characters like Rambo and Rocky.

His self-improvement campaign extended beyond developing verbal and physical skills. He even began a crude form of self-therapy for his atrophied face muscles. He would stand in front of the mirror and force his drooping lower lip into a smile so people would stop being intimidated by an unintended snarl. 'But instead,' he said of this amateur physical therapy, 'it looked like I'd sucked on a lemon or was about to tell a lie.' His peers remained unimpressed and continued their taunts. 'I was the original Elephant Man. I only learned to smile a couple of years ago,' he said in 1990, only half-joking.

While cruel, his father's denigration of his son's mental capacities was based on experience. The youth was a straight F student. Years later, his academic deficiencies would be explained by Attention Deficit Disorder, a learning disability which makes it almost impossible for the afflicted to focus or retain information. Today, there are special classes and exercises to compensate for this disorder which scientists suspect is organic. Some attribute it to brain trauma; others to a vitamin deficiency during a child's early years. Considering Stallone's birth trauma and his diet-induced rickets, either hypothesis might have caused his ADD. In the '50s, however, undiagnosed sufferers were just called 'dumb' and told to compensate with muscles.

Or maybe his imagination, which would later create hugely successful screenplays, was just too overripe for the pedestrian tastes of his teachers. A 400-word essay Stallone wrote described what it would be like to eat a car. His teacher scrawled an 'F' on the paper with the comment, 'but you can't eat a car'. Stallone's colourful mind refused to be ground down by lesser imaginations. He replied, 'But what if you *could* eat a car?'

Unfortunately, his inventiveness also took less productive forms. He later said he was in danger of becoming a 'JD' – years after the fact still finding it difficult to say 'juvenile delinquent'. At 13, he borrowed his father's car and crashed it. 'I played chicken with cars. I even played it with trains,' he said, again probably in myth-mode.

He was kicked out of parochial and public schools in both Philadelphia and Maryland. A Catholic school in Maryland allegedly bounced him for eating the nuns' desserts and hiding their crucifixes, which sounds more like the adult Stallone's self-mythmaking than childhood history. Other causes of expulsion allegedly included hacking up a statue of Santa Claus and shooting arrows out of a classroom window.

(Also add to the 'Apocrypha File' his claim that a placement test he took recommended an unpromising career path – up and down! A test that he alleged had been administered by the Drexel Institute of Technology in Philadelphia concluded that 'the subject was suited to work in the area of elevator operations. In other words, I'd be the guy who crawls through the trap door of an elevator to tighten the cables.' More likely, Stallone was reporting fact, not myth when he added, 'I was told by teachers that my brain was dormant and I took it to heart.')

Three public schools in Philadelphia expelled him for setting fire to trashcans and knocking kids unconscious who criticised his physical handicaps or unusual first name. But as his muscles and knockouts grew, the taunts diminished and gradually ended. Stallone learned an inappropriate message that would years later make great movies but cause problems with personal and professional relationships: 'Let your fists do the talking.'

Despite her son's bad behaviour, his mother was delighted he had found a productive channel for his energies and gave him a set of weights to take home from the gym. Weight-training improved his athletic abilities in other areas, and the once loner tried out and made the track team at Lincoln High in Philadelphia where, despite disproportionately short legs, he managed to set records.

While his athletic prowess increased, his academic performance got even worse, if there's such a thing as an F-minus. By 16, Stallone had been in 20 schools, bounced from most for disciplinary problems. He toyed with the idea of dropping out of school and entering the Navy, but his father discouraged him, saying his son would find military discipline even more unacceptable than school. It apparently never occurred to the older Stallone that a stint in the armed services would do what it has done for so many other delinquents – force them to mature and become responsible young men. Instead, Frank Sr invited him to join the family business, hairdressing.

Amazingly, the rebellious youth agreed, but came to regret the six months of torture he spent teasing women's hair. He soon realised, 'Oh, boy! This work isn't for me! I was worse than the Butcher of Seville. A woman would come in with seven hairs on her head and tell me to make her beautiful. I'd say, "You ever tried a head transplant?" He finally fled the salon on the day he had to learn pincurl and finger-waving techniques, whatever those are. Fleeing his dad's Maryland salon, Stallone returned to mom and high school in Philadelphia.

Jacqueline decided her son's problems couldn't be cured with barbells and increased self-esteem. Muscle development made him feel better about himself, but hadn't diminished his truancy. Maybe an expensive private school for problem kids would help. She found just the place at Manor High School, run by the Devereux Foundation in Berwyn, a suburb of Philadelphia.

Founded in 1950 and still in business, Manor described its goals in a school brochure. Its philosophy sounded tailor-made for coping with Stallone's problems. Manor's aim was 'to provide a normalising private school experience in a therapeutic atmosphere of understanding and open communication in which a student can develop into a productive individual able to function successfully in college, a career or in the community'. Its student body possessed 'an intellectual level from average to very superior and *exhibited a wide range of emotional problems.*'

The co-ed facility sprawled over 30 lush acres and its enrolment was limited to only 100 students, so each troubled youth could receive the care and attention necessary for kids with behavioural and emotional problems, of which Stallone had a lot. Students were required to meet weekly with a psychotherapist for one-on-one sessions plus group therapy. In addition, after years of humiliation and embarrassment, Stallone began speech therapy. As his slurred speech improved, so did his social skills and self-confidence.

Stallone changed his name to Mike when he enrolled at Manor High, and for the first time in his life, he didn't have to deal with peers making fun of his unusual first name. Also, none of the students made fun of his less noticeable speech impediment, or his droopy facial features. Under the nurturing influence of Manor's therapeutic environment, Stallone blossomed again. At the gym, his body had helped diminish his sense of physical inadequacy. At his new school, athletics transformed him from a loner to a joiner. He made the fencing, boxing, equestrian and football teams, playing full-back the year Manor won the conference-title championship. The former loner became popular enough to win election as co-captain of the team.

The caption under his senior yearbook photograph suggests how much Manor had transformed the former bad boy. Calling him by his new name, the yearbook said, 'Mike is one of the most popular boys in school. This is the result of his good nature and excellent compatability. Among other superlatives mentioned, Mike is an excellent athlete. This past year he was co-captain of the football team. Mike is an ardent sports enthusiast and never ceases to be found arguing for the Eagles [the name of Manor's sports teams]. As for the future, Mike hopes to attend college and succeed in all ventures.' Under 'Activities', the yearbook suggests the former truant not only came to class but spent a lot of time after school as well: 'Yearbook (4) [senior year], Football (3,4), Track (3,4), Varsity Club.'

The yearbook also lists his home address as 2744 Mowes Street, Philadelphia, PA, which meant he was living with his mother during his senior year. Life with mom was better than the alternating year with dad, but apparently not without criticism in both homes. Years later, Jacqueline not only continued to humiliate her son, but she did so with stories her son flat out called lies. Jackie told *Sports Illustrated* in 1990, 'Sly desperately wanted to play football, but his grades were so bad they wouldn't let him on the team. So one day I drive by his high school during practice and see him in a uniform, leaping up and down outside the fence. He's borrowed the uniform so everyone will think he's a player. I think, how pathetic! He just wants to be accepted, and he's acting like a clown.'

In all the other published interviews I read in researching this book, I never found a quote in which the star criticised his mother, except for the following, which *Sports Illustrated* inserted immediately after his mother's allegation that he pretended to be on the football team. The respected sports magazine reported: 'Stallone snorts at his mother's story. "That's all made up. She tries to make up my whole past. She tells people she taught me how to box." He smiles sardonically.' Sardonically or sadly?

Manor High turned out to be a genuine curative for the footloose youth. He spent two years there and graduated, something his parents thought would never happen to the chronic truant. The 'cure', however, didn't come too cheap and to their credit after years of self-absorption and neglect, his parents spent a whopping $20,000 on their son's tuition.

Manor wasn't all athletics and improved attendance. While there, Stallone lost his virginity, although the details have none of the 'first-time' glow of many youthful encounters. In fact, they sound downright creepy! Stallone chose the wrong girl for his deflowering. She had a full-time boyfriend, but apparently she found the muscular football star appealing enough to cheat on her regular beau. The boyfriend followed the two to their trysting place and waited until the couple were *in flagrante delicto* to break it up. It was a unique 'first time' in many ways, and not just the usual. Stallone found himself in a fistfight in the nude. The school punished him not only for illicit sex, but for fighting undressed!

That account, however, conflicts with another tale Stallone tells about his other 'first' time. Maybe you can lose your virginity twice – at least in the fantasy land of revisionist celebrity autobiography. On another occasion, Stallone claimed his introduction to sex occurred when he was a *pre*-teen. This time, there was no fight with a jealous boyfriend, but Stallone's first time on this occasion could have used some drama, since the object of his lust barely registered a pulse. 'I was about 12, which, back then, was rather advanced. My friends didn't learn anything about *anything* until they were 14 to 16, forget about actually having sex, which came usually when you were like 17 or 18. Today, you've been married twice by then. My first time was with a beautiful person whom I was completely immobilised by. Her name was Ingrid, a wonderful person because she had no personality at all. The kind of person that you'd put a mirror under her nose to see if she was breathing. She inherited all these lovely physical attributes with no mental stimulus whatsoever. Flypaper was more interesting to hang out with. Social graces and the ability to communicate weren't very high on my list back then.'

His sexual initiation left him with a lifelong distrust of women and a belief in the impermanence of relationships, an ethos that would haunt him through three marriages and enough failed liaisons to make Don Juan blush or Casanova suggest a 12-step programme for sexual addiction.

'Ingrid sent me crashing to earth. The day after she and I got together, she was off with Joey Bambatts, then kept on going to Eddie Mannuno, then to 'Zig' Bruno and worked her way through the whole school. I was just a key on her giant xylophone of love.

'And you know what? *Nothing's changed.* Sure, the wardrobe changes and the locale, but the interaction is still the same. I don't care how much money you make or that you deal on a more intellectual, so-called "spiritual level" as you grow up. The very same kind of romantic tragedies and maladies still occur.'

Despite his athletic record, his academic record made college a near impossibility. Again, Jacqueline poured her energy into helping her son, but even her Herculean efforts were to no avail. Basically, no American university would take a student with a 0.0 average. His mother wasn't discouraged and took her search abroad, where she finally found a place willing to take such a poor prospect.

Her far-flung research discovered that the American College in Leysin, Switzerland, was strapped for cash. The school had originally rejected her son for the same reason its American counterparts had but, like Don Corleone, Jacqueline made them a deal the financially besieged school found impossible to refuse. Flying to Switzerland, she volunteered to write out a cheque for a full-year's tuition in advance. If her son flunked out, the school could keep the money. Amazingly, this worked. To help with expenses, however, the school agreed to grant her son a working scholarship. In return for room and board, Stallone became the college's boxing coach.

The tuition deal was just one story Jacqueline Stallone propagated after her son's success in Hollywood made him the source of intense public interest. Another tale she likes to tell claims she flew to Switzerland, but instead of a cheque for tuition, she charmed the president of the college by casting his horoscope.

Years later, Stallone didn't credit his mother's intervention. He explained his admission to the American College by saying, 'They were taking trolls. That's how desperate they were. All of a sudden, I'm on a mountaintop. And I'm going "What did I do wrong?" I thought I'd been in a plane crash and died.'

Maybe it *was* the altitude and clear mountain air, but college had a tonic effect on him. It was like a cerebral version of his mother's gym. Or maybe it was the clean air at 4,500 feet, where the school nestled at the foot of the Alps. After years of failure, Stallone turned himself around academically. He earned passing grades in mathematics, science and history. And for the first time in his life, he actually excelled at two subjects: art and literature. The composition teachers at this school felt a mind so inventive it could imagine the taste of eating an automobile was something to be encouraged, not flunked. Stallone's favourite novelists at this time were John Dos Passos and Ernest Hemingway.

College encouraged him enough to embark on a full-scale self-improvement regimen – a dramatic makeover to make up for his early years of self-loathing. Stallone began painting and writing poetry. Instead of stuffing his mouth with pebbles like another famous verbally challenged victim, Demosthenes, Stallone read Shakespeare and Walt Whitman out loud into a tape recorder to chart his progress.

Her son's improved literary tastes delighted his mother. She was so big on the importance of reading that when she caught her son reading porn, instead of hitting the ceiling, she professed herself delighted that at least he was reading *something*!

Jacqueline's tolerance toward X-rated literature wasn't surprising since she took it upon herself to teach her son about the birds and the bees rather than risk her husband warping his son's introduction to the subject. Upfront as she was about everything else, Jackie didn't bother with euphemisms about insects' mating rituals. She went straight to the heart of the matter, although other parts of the anatomy were more important in her sex lectures.

Her son recalled, 'From early on, I've always been extremely attracted to the opposite sex and was extremely aggressive in that way. When [his mother] figured that out, she sat me down and she didn't pull any punches. I was aghast at how graphic she got. She skipped right over the birds, the bees and the bears and went straight to, "There's a woman, a man" – like it was a heifer and a bull – "and they slam ham."'

If Stallone came out his shell at Manor High, he took flight at the American College, joining the Drama Club and the Social Service Club. A hint of his popularity with the opposite sex comes from the 1966 yearbook entry which said his nickname on campus was 'Studly'!

His new-found ability to fit in was all the more remarkable since his background was so different from most of his peers. An exclusive school, the American College had a tiny enrolment of only 300, most of whom came from wealthy families, even royalty. Somehow, a youngster who had once felt so dislocated he wore Superboy drag and fantasised about Steve Reeves managed to not only fit in but become popular among rich brats and richer royals. The street kid from Hell's Kitchen and Philadelphia's tough Northeast side hobnobbed with heirs to industrial fortunes and became best buds and business partner with a real-life prince.

Maybe Stallone had developed his empathy skills after so many years of being pummelled during his scrawny youth. As a boxing coach with biceps of steel and a killer hook, he never worried about assaults anymore and even found himself protecting weaker students – including Prince Paul of Ethiopia, whom he rescued during a brawl at school. Like a fairy tale after the nightmare of Stallone's youth, the handsome prince showered the pug with expensive gifts and even bankrolled his outlandish scheme to introduce McDonalds-style fastfood to Switzerland. Stallone and His Royal Highness peddled what they called '*vache*burgers' to the students out of the garage of a rented chalet. If ever there was a case of false advertising and deceptive labeling, the duo's 'cowburgers' were just that. The 'beef' was actually horsemeat, lamb and, according to the chef, 'sawdust'.

Stallone soon found less larcenous but more rewarding outlets for his entrepreneurial ambitions. He landed a job as monitor of the girls' dormitory at the American College. His chief duty was to keep boys out of the girls' dorm, where his imposing physique and martial arts skills proved invaluable. But his success left the field open for him. Or as he put it, 'It was like leaving the fox in charge of the henhouse.' And again, his business sense overcame his sense of responsibility. Stallone began charging the college boys two francs apiece to peek into the girls' dormitory. He also took bribes from their boyfriends to let them spend the night in the dorm.

Field trips with his charges provided another bonanza.

Assigned to chaperone the co-eds on a trip to Paris, Stallone pocketed the money given him for a hotel and put the girls up in a fleabag youth hostel. His aim was selfless, he later said tongue-in-cheek. The girls got to see the 'real' Paris. Or at least the view from a grimy hotel window.

He found another way to supplement his income – or so he claimed years later. Stallone taught students how to fake asthma attacks so they could dodge the gym requirement. Lessons started at $20 a pop and were more popular than the *vache*burgers.

While the American College in Leysin introduced him to literature, new friends and lots of romance, it also infected him with the acting bug, a lifelong virus that still torments and delights him. Amazingly, the former thick-tongued youth auditioned and landed the role of Biff, the underachiever son of Willy Loman in a campus production of *Death of a Salesman*.

'It was an accident,' he said of this pivotal event in his search for self-acceptance. 'I was walking down a hallway, and they were auditioning for *Death of a Salesman*. And, for God knows what reason, I walked in and read for the part of Biff. I couldn't believe it when I got it. That was it for me. It gave me a focus, a direction – if you're gonna be a failure, at least be one at something you enjoy. And I was a great failure for years.' For once, Stallone is not mythologising about how long he paid his dues as a struggling actor. But that's another nightmare for another chapter.

Insults and assaults at home and school gave way to applause on stage. The theatre – and later the movies – would turn out to be Stallone's favourite place to be. The gym improved his body image. The approbation of an audience was even more intoxicating and tonic. The standing ovation on the opening night of *Death of a Salesman* convinced him he had finally found his place in a universe that had previously rejected him physically and mentally. 'I thought, "This is it! I've finally done something right! From here on in, I'm going for it."'

Stallone could show on stage all the emotions which when expressed in real life got him expelled from school or worse. A cathartic scene in *Death of a Salesman* was his favourite. Biff offers his mother a bouquet of flowers, which she rejects because he's left his drunken father in a bar. The script called for him to hurl the bouquet against the wall. One night, however, his emotions overwhelmed him and he decided to improvise – disastrously. Not just the flowers, but a radio was heaved at the wall of the set by the former champion high school discus thrower. The 'wall' was actually made of canvas, and it collapsed, revealing the stagehands, 'drinking beer, puffing on "hot dogs" [marijuana] and sniffing glue! It was a comedy sensation,' Stallone said. Unrecorded were the feelings of the play's director at finding the greatest American tragedy of the twentieth century turned into a 'comedy sensation'.

The Alps, however, were not the part of the universe best suited to launch an acting career, so in 1967, after two years of hustling horsemeat and finding a new life in the theatre, he left the American College in Leysin and enrolled in the University of Miami as – what else? – a theatre major.

# Chapter Two

# Back in the Not So Good Old US of A

If the young actor hoped to recreate his Alpine stage experience – standing ovations in a major play and a showcase supporting role like Biff – he was quickly disillusioned back in America. The University of Miami hated him. Or at least the drama department did. 'Stink' was actually the word the university casting people used. It was like being back in grade school and forced to strip down to his secret Superboy togs – emotionally if not literally.

'It was the most emotionally crippling experience I ever had,' he said of Miami U. 'They were saying to me, "Quit! You stink! You're bad!" I succumbed to depression, then decided to fight back.'

It wasn't just his acting talent but his choice of subject matter that turned off the drama school faculty. Just as he would years later battle with studios and directors over script control, Stallone wanted to be the drama department's artistic director. He longed to do experimental theatre. The faculty, on the other hand, saw a Steve Reeves clone attempting Albee and Ionesco.

His teachers considered him 'too aggressive, too mannered, too physical to act,' Stallone said. It didn't help that he only looked qualified for gladiator epics, not neurotic guys who turn into rhinoceroses or stab their foreign language students during a private tutorial. 'At that time, I was very heavily into bodybuilding. It came from deep-rooted insecurity. You kind of create a muscular shell to protect that soft inside. You try to build yourself into the image that you think people will respect, and it tends to get a little extreme. It's like playing God, rebuilding your body in your own image,' or in reaction to childhood taunts from classmates and parent.

The drama professors at Miami didn't really care about the psychological underpinnings of his muscular superstructure. They wanted lean, not beefcake. Also, some teachers felt his diminished speech impediment was still, well, a stage impediment for projecting to the back of the theatre. One helpful drama coach told him to lose the muscles because Annette Funicello and Frankie Avalon 'muscle beach movies had run their course', he said.

Instead of fighting back with his fists or bombing horseflies with bricks on the hood of his father's car, Stallone found a more passive way to combat the rejection, although these attempts were as futile as his efforts at insect control. He immersed himself in the oeuvres of the Theatre of the Absurd, Albee and Ionesco, Becket and Genet. Alas, by 1967, the existentialists were as out of favour as Frankie and Annette.

With off off-Broadway playwrights like Israel Horovitz as his culture heroes – a major artistic distancing from Steve Reeves's dubbed dialogue – Stallone began compulsively writing very avant-garde playlets. Miami's theatre department hated the avant-garde even more than his bulging arms. Forget about mounting a production of *The Bald Rhinoceros* – a play by Sylvester Stallone. The faculty wouldn't even let him read from his plays to audition for the more run-of-the-mill stuff the middle-brow college favoured.

Disillusioned, Stallone tried to fall back on what he thought would be a sure-thing: his muscles and athletic prowess. He tried out for the football team, the scene of his high school glory, and was rejected there too. The sports department didn't want his body; the drama department didn't want his mind – especially its feverish outpourings of the no longer 'avant' avant-garde!

When someone put a roadblock in front of him, Stallone rarely went around it. He crashed right through. If the university wouldn't give him a role or a venue for his plays, he'd create his own theatre! He produced and starred in his plays in garages, church basements and anywhere else in the city where the rent was cheap. He even created a small troupe of actors and put on the works of real avant-gardeists like Israel Horovitz's *Rats*.

Stallone claimed he was so 'hands-on' with every element of these productions he even managed to get the school newspaper to run reviews he secretly wrote himself. One blurb he remembered years later: 'John Herzfeld [a co-writer] and Sylvester Stallone exploded onto the stage like whirling Tasmanian dervishes!'

The acceptance – and applause – of these tiny church basement/garage audiences had a pivotal effect on Stallone's career, or at least on his self-confidence. His success in these beyond Broadway showcases gave him the confidence to ignore his college teachers and realise he had something to offer, acting and writing skills.

Three credits short of a college degree, Stallone dropped out of the University of Miami and moved to New York City, his first home and the traditional place for actors to starve. His new surroundings would make his parents' cold-water flat in Hell's Kitchen seem luxurious by comparison.

But before hitting the Great White Way – or his slum apartment – there was an emotional reunion with his mother, who had spent a fortune and lots of time getting her son into college, only to see him become a dropout so close to the great American dream of a college diploma. Before New York, he stopped off in Philadelphia, where Jackie decided to deal with her son's failure in a positive way. She cast his horoscope. It was a case of good news/bad news, if you believe in the Zodiac. Both mother and son did. Their belief in the bogus science of astrology, however pooh-poohed by real scientists, had a salutary effect on his career.

Based on the chart she cast for her son, Stallone would achieve enormous success! That was the good news. Not so good: it would take seven years for this miracle to happen. And worst, success would come as a writer, not as an actor. After the wholesale rejection of Stallone as both actor and writer at the University of Miami, Jackie's prediction had more the flavour of a curse than an encouraging omen. But the optimistic young man believed his mother. Maybe because the alternative – a lifetime of failure – was too unpalatable to believe.

At least he had practice as a writer – from 400-word essays on auto cuisine to *Genet*-ic playlets. Stallone eventually realised, however, that the avant-garde was going nowhere, so he decided to try naturalism and that style's best exemplar, the screenplay.

He rented a room at the Sutton Hotel, which he nicknamed the 'Slutton' for reasons he never explained in an interview years later with the *New York Times*, although considering its proximity to Times Square's red light district, maybe the actor felt his pun self-explanatory.

His one-room apartment sounds more like an 'insufficiency' rather than a sufficiency. There was insufficient space to do just about anything but write his heart out. The room was so Lilliputian 'you could lie in your bed and stretch out your arms and open the door, shut the window, turn on a faucet. You never had to move.' The rats, he said, had bigger arms than he did.

The claustrophobia somehow tweaked his Muse, however, or maybe the dismal surroundings forced him to retreat into the fantasy world of writing because reality was so ugly. Plus, he wasn't impressed with what was out there. 'I saw *Easy Rider*, and I figured I couldn't write any worse.' Years later, he'd admit that he could and did do worse with his early screenplays.

Stallone bought a how-to book on screenwriting and sat down to write The Great American Screenplay. His obsession isolated him socially, but the lack of social life made him productive and prolific. In fact, despite the hellish surroundings and rejection, Stallone claims he was happy during this super-creative period in his life. 'I wasn't very gregarious, though. Didn't party. Ninety per cent of my time was in the workplace. Always driving, driving . . . '

His first effort was *Cry Full, Whisper Empty, In the Same Breath*.

Stallone sent his script to producers and agents – and it was returned unread. In retrospect, he didn't blame them because 'it *was* really awful,' he said.

His second stab at writing was titled *Sad Blues*. Stallone allegedly based it on the career of his aspiring pop star brother, Frank Jr, although the ending, fortunately, was not biographical. *Sad Blues* lived up to its title as the tale of a down and out singer with a heart condition who believes only bananas can cure him. Stallone obviously was reverting to his Theatre of the Absurd inclinations here, despite the fact that he was writing screenplays, not one-act plays in the basements of Miami *iglesias*. At the climax, the hero goes onstage without taking his daily dose of bananas. He collapses and his girlfriend, who has earlier dumped him, tries to revive him by shoving a banana down his throat, but it's too late. The wannabe popstar dies on stage in his ex-lover's arms.

His second screenplay met the same bewildered rejection, but nothing could discourage the writer, since after all, his mother had assured him that that was where success ultimately lay.

He composed his third screenplay, *Till Young Men Exit*, on scraps of paper torn from legal notepads. The plot was high concept and much more commercial than the ones about potassium deficiency and whatever *Cry Full Whisper* . . . was about. (All these early efforts, sadly, have been lost to would-be archivists of the Stallone *oeuvre*.)

*Till Young Men Exit* was also a bit autobiographical, although purely fantasy – fortunately. A group of unsuccessful actors take hostage a Broadway producer as an alternative to yet another fruitless audition. 'Gimme the part or else, buddy!' Unfortunately, the impresario dies, like the pop star in *Sad Blues*, due to poor diet. The actors must be *very* angry, because the producer is forced to live – and ultimately perish – on a diet of Fizzies and Kool-Aid.

Just in case his mom's crystal ball and chart were wrong, Stallone continued to bust his chops as an actor. Without a union card, he could only go to open auditions, also known as cattle calls. The same phrase to describe his persona kept coming up during these auditions. Everyone said he was a 'Marlon Brando' type. The muscles, the tight T-shirts, the mumbling – all gave credence to the analogy but didn't land him any roles. There were hundreds, if not thousands, of actors 'doing' Brando on both coasts . . . when they weren't waiting tables or tending bar.

One audition suggests how maddening these cattle calls had become – and how mad Stallone could get. Movie star Sal Mineo (*Rebel Without a Cause*) was casting an off Broadway production of *The Fortune in Men's Eyes*, which he would later recast in Los Angeles with a then unknown named Don Johnson. The play, considered a minor classic, takes place in a prison, with a gruesome rape scene. It's testimony to how desperate Stallone was for a gig at this time that the raging heterosexual would consider being so cast against type.

Typically, he threw himself into the audition anyway, hurling chairs – and even stage crew members – under the proscenium. Director Mineo wasn't impressed with his rage and told him he didn't seem angry enough to play a con!

Those were fighting words for a young man who had plenty of the real thing bottled up inside, and he decided the audition was a great place to uncork all the resentments caused by a lifetime of abuse and rejections, personally and professionally. Stallone rushed the director, stopping a few millimetres from his nose and screamed, 'Tell me I'm not intimidating.' Mineo stood his ground, despite the fact that the muscular actor towered over the ectomorphic director. Mineo agreed that Stallone was indeed intimidating, but still refused to cast him as the character, who had the prophetic name of Rocky.

Stallone had to travel to the Bronx for his first acting job in New York. It was something of a coup, the role of the Minotaur in Picasso's only play, *Desire Caught by the Tail*, even though it only ran three weeks. Audiences averaged ten or less per performance. Stallone found himself literally suffering for his art, and we're not talking about his one-room apartment at the Slutton. One night, an over imaginative co-star decided to kill the monstrous Minotaur by spraying Stallone full in the face with a fire extinguisher. The carbon dioxide filled his lungs and he ended up in the emergency room, where he joked that his face had to be defrosted with a heat lamp.

By now, as an actor, Stallone wasn't just paying his dues . . . he was paying the physical and psychological equivalent of extortion money. His parents were both affluent by this time, but after years of being told he was a loser by dad and wasting his mother's efforts for her son's higher education, Stallone was too proud to ask for rent money. He moved out of the Sutton in early 1970 and became homeless.

Stallone kept warm like thousands of other down and outers at the Port Authority Bus Terminal on New York's bombed out 42nd Street. A great place for the name of a musical, a nightmare name for a 'home' address. At this time, he says he was literally a 'starving actor'. His last quarter was spent not on food but on a locker at the bus station to store the tools of his craft – pencils, notebooks and books on acting theory and screenwriting.

At the library he found free copies of the trades and caught an announcement for yet another open audition. But instead of an icky little off-Broadway play about prison rape, he'd be auditioning for a movie role.

Unfortunately, it was a porn movie, *Party at Kitty and Studs*. Stallone went 'up' for the title role, which he got. His first legit job, if that's the right word for the subterranean world of porn. Actually, *Kitty and Studs* was really *soft* porn, literally. As stills published in *Playgirl* magazine 15 years later show, none of the men were aroused (maybe it was the dialogue that was so unarousing). No erections and definitely no penetration. Today, the film would get an anxious 18 certificate.

During the audition, the producers asked if he would have a problem with nudity. 'They wanted to know if I'd take off my clothes! I said, "Why not? I take them off for free every night!"' Stallone said. This time, however, he'd be paid $100 a day to disrobe, a fortune for the starving actor who said of these days of struggling, 'I was cold and sick and broke and on the very brink of committing a criminal act . . . it was either do the movie or rob someone.'

The minimalist plot of *Kitty and Studs* sounds more

amateurish than Stallone's screenplays at this time. Stud (Stallone) posts a notice on a bulletin board inviting people to participate in an orgy. Four people RSVP. The movie contains the obligatory shower scene, with his leading lady urging him to bend over and pick up the soap — the heterosexual version of *Fortune and Men's Eyes*.

Less typical of porn, the entire cast joins in a nude 'ring-a-roses' dance. Photos in *Playgirl* in 1985 are fascinating . . . and not just because they give us a peek at a future superstar. As the nine-page spread in the October issue shows, Stallone was indeed a 'starving' actor – or at least a guy who wasn't eating enough. Gone were the 16-inch arms in the snapshots of his teen years. Another still which shows a double-bicep pose is embarrassing, not because of the nudity, since he's wearing a bath towel, but because he has very little to flex in front of the mirror.

Steve Reeves had been his boyhood idol and role model, whom he emulated by trying to duplicate the star's Herculean physique. There's a psychological cliché that bodybuilders often overcompensate with brawn for what they lack in, uh, endowment. Without being cruel, let's just say the *Playgirl* photo where he doesn't wear a towel suggests the cliché is a truism.

Today, Stallone says about *Party at Kitty and Studs*: 'There wasn't any hardcore stuff, so what did I care? At the time I made it, it was the solution to a problem, which was that I was starving and broke.'

Indeed, *no one* cared about the film, which couldn't find a distributor until years later, when 'Studs' became 'Rocky Balboa'. The producers offered the negative to the new superstar for $100,000. Stallone refused to give in to what amounted to extortion, even when the producers retitled the film, *The Italian Stallion* and offered 'private screenings' at parties for $10,000 a pop. 'I don't think the movie was ever released,' he said inaccurately in 1977. 'Today the parasitical maggots who made it are trying to market that piece of scum. They want $100,000.' Stallone was charmed rather than alarmed by the subtle extortion attempt. 'Hell, for $100,000, forget the film. I'll be there myself.' After its theatrical run, *The Italian Stallion* became a sellout at video stores, where it's still available for connoisseurs who want to see the entire Stallone canon.

While his first screen effort paid $100 *per diem*, the shoot only lasted two days. But with two hundred bucks he was able to move off the streets and into $71-a-month flat above an abandoned delicatessen on 56th Street and Lexington. The walkup made the Slutton seem like Sutton Place. He was no longer homeless, although the bus terminal sounds almost more commodious. Referring to his vermin-infested pad, Stallone joked he was subletting to cockroaches who took over the bathtub and toilet, making them virtually unusable.

The place was rented unfurnished, and that's the way it stayed. Stallone used an apple crate as his writing desk. His overcoat served as bed, blanket and sheets. He 'did the laundry' by showering with his clothes on.

Stallone's day jobs were as hellish as his night-time resting place. He sliced open fish at a Manhattan delicatessen and delivered pizzas before being promoted to pizza-maker. Cleaning out the lion's cage at New York's Central Park Zoo paid $1.12 an hour and didn't begin to cover drycleaning costs when a lion urinated on his one pair of trousers, which were beyond the services of his shower/laundromat. 'Let me tell you,' he said of the irreverent cats, 'they're accurate up to 15 feet!' No amount of laundering could get rid of the smell, which turned out to be a weird blessing. Stallone smelled so bad he always got a seat on the subway. One whiff and the other passengers fled as far as the next car!

Auditions were as humiliating as his day jobs, with the added feature of cruelty. Despite a lopsided, self-described 'snarl' caused by his birth injury, his witless agent sent him to read for a toothpaste commercial. The casting director took one look and asked, 'What did you do, just kill a baby?'

Like the apocryphal story of the actor told he was too ugly to play Quasimodo, Stallone found himself being rejected for roles that amounted to typecasting. His sometime agent Rhonda Young remembered, 'I sent him to [an] Ivory Soap [audition].

They were looking for a greaser, but they sent him back. They said there was a limit to seediness!'

Stallone also got a break on his rent by working as his building's 'super', although he described the job of superintendent as 'bouncer', specifically, bouncing the homeless people who collected in and around the place. 'It was my job to oust the bums and beggars who slept in the lobby and halls,' which pained the soft-hearted young man, since he himself only a short while earlier had used the bus station for the same purpose. 'For good luck, I used to drop a coin in one of their tin plates before going in for an audition. It became a habit.' Years later, Stallone had second thoughts about his penny-ante philanthropy when he returned to his 'roots' and found the same guys still homeless. 'It wasn't right, because every time you give beggars money, you're only reinforcing their problem. You're making it so they don't have to go to work.' That was Stallone's head talking. His heart still bled for these unfortunates. Ignoring his own 'pull yourself up by the bootstraps' theory of economics, he later gave a panhandler a handout and was shocked when the man wished *him*, a zillionaire superstar, 'good luck'.

One of his less repellent jobs would also have a profound influence on his life and career. Stallone became an usher at the Baronet Theatre, the flagship of the Walter Reade movie chain. Every major film premièred there, and people anxious to get in on opening night would queue up even in New York's inclement weather. Stallone began scalping tickets, whispering to movie-goers he could sneak them in ahead of everyone else for only five bucks. So many people paid up, the young man was soon pocketing $300 to $600 a week, a fortune in 1970.

His windfall abruptly ended the night *M\*A\*S\*H* premiered at the Baronet. Stallone saw an expensively dressed elderly gentlemen in a white suit with a red carnation in his lapel and immediately upped his asking fee. 'Hey, for 20 bucks I can get you a good seat!' It was an offer the nattily attired man found easy to refuse. He even made a counter-offer. 'Hey, for *nothing* I can get you your walking papers. I'm Walter Reade!'

Stallone was fired on the spot. But not before he met a fellow-employee who would change his life and give him two children, serve as his amanuensis, cheerleader and emotional supporter for life.

Sasha Czach, originally from Chester, Pennsylvania, worked in the Baronet Theatre's ticket booth. She was petite, blonde and gorgeous. Stallone said he fell instantly in love when he saw the aspiring actress dispensing tickets from her glass-enclosed 'shrine'. Wearing a greasy sheepskin jacket 'so old it leaked; I had to put Vaseline on it to keep it waterproofed' and shoulder-length hair almost as greasy, Stallone introduced himself in a way that hardly qualified him as Mr Smooth and turned off the object of his infatuation. 'I think I love you,' he said through the little metal grill in the glass ticket booth.

Stallone later justified his come on. He was too broke to make a more traditional offer, like going on a date. 'Who could afford a social life?' he said. 'You couldn't say to some girl, "Hey, let's go to the park." She'd say, "But it's snowing."'

More than a decade and a half later, Stallone could remember all the details down to the seductive clothing that still enraptured him. 'She was taking tickets at the Baronet and wearing a lowcut black thing – they dressed the usherettes that way to entice people in.' It took him a year after their first meeting to entice her to move into his apartment. In the meantime, he pursued his career as vigorously as he courted Sasha.

After a series of dead-end jobs and soul-deadening auditions that would have killed a less tenacious soul, in the summer of 1970 Stallone got a bit of encouragement that perhaps he was on the right track after all.

A few years earlier, the all-singing, all-dancing, all *nude* cast of *Oh, Calcutta!* had made nude musicals an art form. Ironically, Stallone's first 'movie break' had him stripping in a porn flick. His first legitimate off-Broadway gig would require the same, plus acting skill, which he demonstrated first to the director of *Score* and then delighted theatre critics.

*Score* tapped into the 'swinging single' craze of the '60s and '70s before AIDS expanded the term to 'swinging . . . from the end of a rope' a decade later. *Score*, eerily like *Party at Kitty and*

*Studs*, involved a 'four-way', two married couples. The sex quartet turns into a quintet when they invite a telephone repairman who shows up to fix the phone to take a break from his job and join in.

Stallone played the repairman in an original variation on 'phone sex'. He was asked to disrobe for the audition, which he did. During the reading, the writer-director, Jerry Douglas, liked what he heard – and, just as importantly, what he saw. 'He gave a good audition and also happened to have a good body,' Douglas said. The choice came down to two actors, and Douglas picked Stallone for his 'charisma'. Plus a 'good body was essential for the part', Douglas said.

Unlike the temperamental superstar of later years, the novice was eager to please and take directions. Douglas said he was 'a dream' to work with, 'creative and very professional'. With hundred million dollar grossing movies to back him up, Stallone would one day become infamous for rewriting other writers' scripts, and Douglas sensed the novice felt the play was pap rather than Papp. But Stallone was also savvy enough not to screw up his biggest gig to date. 'He was a perfect gentleman. He may not have liked it and may have bitched about it offstage, but his deportment throughout was excellent. Very helpful.'

Stallone received 'featuring' billing under the 'star billing' of the more experienced cast members, Michael Beirne, Claire Wilbur, Lynn Swan and Ben Wilson. Perhaps to compensate, he gussied up his name by listing himself as 'Sylvester E. Stallone' – the 'E' for grandpa Stallone, Enzio.

He also wrote his own bio in the play's brochure. Stallone's talents as a 'creative' writer and self-mythologiser demonstrated themselves early and imaginatively when he wrote in the playbill that Sylvester E. Stallone had spent 'several years in Switzerland, during which he toured the country in such shows as *Death of a Salesman, Who's Afraid of Virginia Woolf, Of Mice and Men* . . . on returning to the United States, he appeared in a multitude of regional and educational theatre productions'.

While all struggling actors embroider their resumés, Stallone created an entire quilt out of whole cloth. His list of film credits was accurate, however, up to a point. By then he had indeed appeared in *Lovers & Other Strangers*, *Klute* and *Bananas*, but in all of them as an extra, except *Bananas*, where he strangled a little old lady in the subway while *Über*-nerd Woody Allen ignores the woman's murder!

The producers of *Score* may have suspected the play would not be a *succes d'estime* because they kept the critics away for 30 days of previews before finally declaring 'opening night' and letting their tormentors take a peek on 28 October 1970, at the Martinque Theatre in New York City.

The producers may have wished they had kept the play 'in previews' indefinitely because scabrous reviews closed it after only 23 post-première performances. The *New York Post*'s Richard Watts called *Score* 'sheer garbage'. That was the kindest cut. Mel Gussow of the *New York Times* said 'beneath the pseudo-sophisticated surface, the play is not very different from a pornographic paperback'. Fortunately, Gussow appeared not to know that one cast member had already starred in a film version of the paperback. One critic was kind – at least to Stallone. The influential entertainment industry trade paper *Variety* said, 'The best performance is given by Sylvester E. Stallone as the comically lecherous, lower-middle-class repairman.'

After *Score* failed to score with audiences or the press, Stallone found himself unemployed, but this time there would no longer be any day jobs in and from hell. In 1971, Sasha moved into his already cramped apartment. Unlike Stallone's mother, who kept treading the boards in pursuit of a career that never happened, Sasha gave up her professional dreams to support her man's. She worked full-time as a waitress so her live-in love could devote himself full-time to acting and writing. And her job meant that at least he was no longer a 'starving' actor, since Sasha's boss allowed her to take home two-day-old left-overs, which they heated up on a hotplate in their kitchen-less apartment. Sasha called the place 'awful', but didn't complain about cooking on a tiny food warmer or washing the dishes (not to mention their clothes) in the bathroom sink or eating on the floor because there was no dining-room table, much less a dining-room.

We never learned how Sasha felt about the décor, even after Stallone painted the windows black to block out distracting sights like hobos and hookers in the alley. He also disconnected the phone, not that agents were calling him with work. Stallone was lucky to have Sasha's presence because in his monk-like quest, he said, 'I disassociated myself from most of my friends.'

Sasha stood by her man. And typed up his scratchings with a 19-cent Bic pen on a yellow legal notepad. When his hands got tired, Stallone would stop writing and dictate dialogue as Sasha typed.

As a writer, Stallone could be as wilful as any actor. Sasha diplomatically suggested that taking dictation sometimes involved taking abuse. Circumspectly, she said about playing Boswell to his Dr Johnson: 'He can be very explosive, especially when he's working on a script, and his temperament requires constant attention.' She put up with the 'explosions' by telling herself that 'the anger wasn't directed at me'.

Heat in the apartment was an on-again-off-again thing, more often off, so Stallone left Sasha to shiver and type while he escaped to a warm library, where he discovered he loved to read . . . especially early American fiction, which he erroneously called 'Puritan literature'. The poems and short stories of the brooding Edgar Allan Poe appealed to the brooding, budding actor-writer, who had a lot to brood about.

He soon went from reading about his spiritual *doppelgänger* to writing a screenplay about his hero – as a starring vehicle of course. And like most starring vehicles, the character would have to be tailored to the star, not the other way around. Stallone's take on Poe sounds more autobiographical than biographical: his interpretation, he said, 'would be a radical departure from the traditional view that he was a grovelling dipsomaniac with iambic pentameter dripping from his lips. I would play him with a great roguish abandon, in the vein of *Tom Jones*.' The eighteenth-century English novel by Henry Fielding, not the twentieth-century Welsh pop star. And in the course of the screenplay, the rogue would evolve into the more traditional figure who left the world too early. 'I can identify with Poe's tragic loss of people, his drive and his loneliness,' Stallone added, again suggesting the autobiographical nature of the role.

A quarter century later, Stallone was still talking about the script and his plans to bring it to the screen, although by then even he realised his muscle god bod would have made it ludicrous to star as the emaciated, tubercular poet, although he still hoped to direct the screenplay. Like Ibsen's *Wild Duck*, the Poe project remains a fantasy in the attic of the superstar's imagination. Literary purists pray it stays there.

Stallone's efforts began to bear fruit, or more accurately, produce income. The loneliest part of an aspiring writer's life is writing in a vacuum with no positive feedback, such as payment for one's work. Stallone got positive reinforcement after writing six 30-minute TV scripts in a single day. He didn't find his speed and productivity as a writer impressive. In fact, he was dismissive of writers who laboured — and belaboured — their work in what they may have considered a labour of love, but he considered masochistic self-indulgence.

'I'm astounded by people who take 18 years to write something. That's how long it took that guy to write *Madame Bovary*. And was that ever on a bestseller list? No. It was a lousy book and it made a lousy movie,' he said, after composing *Rocky* in a three-day marathon. He was right, of course, about the 1953 film starring a ludicrously miscast Jennifer Jones as Mrs B and James Mason as the author, Gustave Flaubert, who did indeed spend almost two decades in pursuit of the *le mot juste*. But Stallone was dead wrong about the 1859 novel. Flaubert found *le mot juste*, lots of them in fact, and *Madame Bovary* remains by critical consensus the greatest novel of the nineteenth century. And because of its scandalous tale of a housewife's promiscuous love life, it *was* a bestseller.

One of Stallone's scripts was bought by TV's *Touch of Evil*, an anthology series starring British actor Anthony Quayle, for $2,500, a huge windfall for the starving actor and his waitressing typist! Stallone later laughed at the grotesque scripts he whipped up for Quayle. 'High concept stuff! I'm talking about a butcher who eats his family. Edgar Allan Poe comes back [from the grave]. The Manchester Monster.' For a while, Sylvester and Sasha could turn off the hotplate and eat out.

The excitement of actually selling a script was diluted at this time by his failure to appear in the film version of *Score*. Director Douglas wanted to transport the stage cast intact to the screen. The film's producer, Radley Metzger, considered Stallone an unknown, which he was, and hired a handsome billboard model for the telephone repairman in the movie. Stallone could console himself with the fact that the film never got a theatrical release. When Stallone became famous and another movie effort, *Party at Kitty and Studs* went on to video Valhalla, producer Metzger must have been kicking himself that he hadn't followed the director's advice, because Stallone's new found fame would have given *Score* a second life on video.

Stallone didn't spend all his time in the darkened apartment or the warm library, writing the Great American Screenplay. Although *Score* flopped, it helped him gain admission to an experimental repertory group called The Extension. Sasha's day-job remained a blessing; while The Extension burnished his resumé, it didn't fatten his bank account. His work with the group went unremunerated, but it was a great showcase, with top New York agents, producers and casting directors turning up for the ensemble's workshops and plays.

At this time, Stallone may have had mixed feelings about his younger brother Frank's career, which was prospering more than his sibling's. Frank had inherited his father's magnificent baritone without dad's paralysing shyness. His pop group, Valentine, for which he composed songs and sang lead, got regular gigs at New York clubs. If Stallone resented his brother's success, he used all his talent as an actor to hide it, because more often than not, there was big brother, seated at the table closest to the stage, wildly applauding after each song. Considering their poisonous relationship with dad, Frank Jr's comment that Sylvester was 'a father figure' suggests what an important role Stallone played in his life at this time. It's a warm relationship that continues to this day, but Sylvester's support has taken much more practical forms than clapping at the end of musical sets – like hiring his brother to write songs for his movies and doing a cameo in a vehicle starring Frank Jr.

In 1972, Stallone couldn't obsess too much about his brother's success since he soon found himself in front of the cameras with no time to worry about sibling rivalry or career-envy. It was another no-budget movie, but this time the production would get a major release and make a dramatic change in his life, geographically and professionally.

## Chapter Three

# Lord of Flatbush

By 1972, the indefatigable optimist was beginning to feel defeated. *Score* had failed to score. His film career consisted of extra work and one bit part. Discouraged, Stallone toyed with the idea of abandoning his writing and acting careers.

In one last seemingly quixotic gesture, he and a friend pooled their non-existent resources to write and star in a Western film called *Horses*, shot on 16mm film, strictly amateurville. The unlikely plot involved a dead cowboy and an Indian who had come back to modern times as 'angels'. Played by Stallone and his co-writer, the duo find the world unliveable and decide to go back where they came from, the cemetery.

Even the wildly realistic dreamer Stallone realised the film would never be released. He intended it as a calling card, something to show casting people what he could do. What it showed, by his own admission, was that the star couldn't act or write. Stallone admitted *Horses* was 'so bad that my parents actually walked out of the room – and they'll normally sit through two hours of flower slides.'

*Horses* proved that you should always track down every lead because you never know where it will lead. *Horses* led Stallone to a pivotal audition. His *Horses* co-star was auditioning for a scholarship to a prestigious acting school and asked Stallone to read with him. The school rejected the friend, but offered Stallone a scholarship. He refused, joking, or perhaps not, that he was through with acting and planned, as his earlier career placement test suggested, to study elevator repair.

Stallone couldn't have known it at the time, but a movie writer-producer had sat in on the college audition and liked what he saw. When Stallone returned to his apartment after the reading, he was surprised to find a telegram from the producer, Stephen Verona. Stallone's phone had been disconnected, and a telegram was the only way the producer could offer him a role in his new film.

*The Lords of Flatbush* looked like another dead end. No budget, no distributor, no stars, and less than the Screen Actors Guild minimum pay, since – surprise! – it wasn't a union production. (His salary was $2,000. While not princely, it could get the phone reconnected and put more food . . . on the floor.) Stallone landed the role of Stanley Rosiello, the over-muscled leader of the title's motorcycle gang. Set in 1957, *The Lords of Flatbush* was a bittersweet nostalgia piece about high school seniors in the blue-collar Flatbush area of Brooklyn.

More than one casting director at this time considered Stallone uncastable, but not Stephen Verona and Martin Davidson, who co-wrote and co-directed the autobiographical script. Directors Verona and Davidson, regardless of their filmmaking talent, which critics questioned when the movie came out, turned out to be *casting* directors of genius. And not just in casting the future superstar of the *Rocky* and *Rambo* series. What others considered a handicap or even deformity – Stallone's semi-paralysed face – the filmmakers considered perfect for the dim-witted and inarticulate Stanley Rosiello. And his overdeveloped physique, which got in the way of leading-man roles, was perfect for a hoodish teenager.

The writer-directors' knack for birthing embyronic talent didn't stop with Stallone. Their other casting coups included Henry Winkler, Perry King and Susan Blakely. While the trio today sounds obscure, within a few years of the film Winkler would become a national figure as 'The Fonz' on the TV sitcom *Happy Days*. Blakely would become the siren of the highly rated mini-series *Rich Man, Poor Man*. And King, while sadly underemployed to the point of invisibility today, would become the star stud of innumerable TV movies, mini-series and weekly series during the '70s and '80s.

Despite the excitement of co-starring in a movie, Stallone must have felt that it was *déjà vu*. Like the unwatchable *Horses*, *The Lords of Flatbush* was also shot on 16mm film. The filmmakers planned to blow up the negative to the commercial 35mm format after showing it to distributors, who would provide the funds to accomplish the expensive upgrade. In the meantime, the project struggled with a budget of $400,000, which sounds like a lot more than it was, since the filmmakers never had the money all at one time. *The Lords of Flatbush* took a *Ben Hur*-like two years to film, stopping and starting when the money ran out and the producers scrambled for more funds. By November 1972, only five weeks into shooting, principal photography halted when the initial investment of $50,000 ran out.

While it was hell on his nerves, the prolonged stop-and-start schedule wreaked even more havoc on Stallone's body. Over a two-year period, the project shut down three times. Stallone came to the set with a perfect gym-toned body. The filmmakers wanted the Incredible Hulk and he obligingly bulked up to 225 pounds, an enormous amount of weight for a kid of five feet ten barely out of puberty. Previously, the single-minded actor had starved for his art. Now Stallone bound himself bingeing for the same purpose. 'I was never without a pint of ice cream in my hand and another one hidden away in a thermal bag tucked inside my motorcycle jacket. I was constantly eating, eating, eating to get this look.'

While Stallone sacrificed his perfect body, the filmmakers sacrifcied their pride to secure funding. Davidson not only showed footage to would-be angels – professional moneymen – but when the project ran out of funds, he and co-writer Verona actually went door to door with a 16mm film projector in Flatbush. Davidson claimed the residents were so proud of his depiction of their much maligned neighbourhood, housewives and their blue-collar husbands would write them a cheque after these very private 'screenings'.

The breaks in filming had some benefits. During one hiatus,

Stallone got the lead in another no-budget film, *No Place to Hide*, as a college radical who must choose between his girlfriend and his plans to blow up a New York City skyscraper. With its preposterous storyline, the film failed to find a distributor for two years. When it finally came out in 1974, the US had pulled out of Vietnam, and radicalism as a film subject had become stale instead of revolutionary. But at least *No Place to Hide* kept him busy while waiting to return to *The Lords of Flatbush*.

The delays in that film gave him an even bigger opportunity which would encourage him in his next, career-making venture. During downtime, Stallone turned his prodigious writing energies toward Stanley, his character in *The Lords of Flatbush*. With the writer-directors' permission, he wrote several scenes, including the one in which his pregnant girlfriend emotionally blackmails him into buying her an over-priced diamond ring. Stallone also wrote a follow-up scene in which the thug threatens to beat up the jeweller if he ever shows his girlfriend an expensive piece of jewellery again! *Time* magazine raved about the engagement scene, calling it the 'best in the movie' when 'Stallone's face goes through a generation of changes'. Instead of being envious, the writer-directors even gave Stallone an 'additional dialogue' credit in the film.

By the time *The Lords of Flatbush* finally wrapped in 1974, the filmmakers found a different climate in Hollywood. A year earlier, another micro-budgeted film about high school seniors, *American Graffiti*, had become a major hit and created a giant maw for similarly themed movies. *The Lords of Flatbush*'s timing was perfect. Instead of having to hustle Brooklyn housewives for completion money, the producers found a willing buyer at Columbia, which purchased distribution rights for $150,000 and a 50/50 split of profits. The studio put more money into the film, including blowing it up to 35mm, and launched a major ad campaign. Unlike *No Place to Hide*, *The Lords of Flatbush* got a major send-off that paid off nicely if not extravagantly. Made for less than half a million dollars, the movie grossed ten times its original budget, $4.2 million.

*Time* magazine not only loved Stallone's writing, it called his performance 'truly exceptional'. Unfortunately, while good notices are good for the soul, they won't pay the rent, and praise in the press didn't automatically translate into a huge career boost. Plans to make a sequel, *Flatbush Abroad*, with an unlikely plot in which Stallone's Stanley and his new bride win a free trip to Europe on the gameshow *Let's Make a Deal*, mercifully never came to fruition. And a TV series based on the film also never happened despite initial interest from the networks because of the success of a similar-themed series, *Happy Days*, which became a huge hit for another *Flatbush* star, Henry Winkler, in a role he generously admitted he based on Stallone's Stanley.

Stallone wasn't unemployed during this downtime, but his career took a step down with his next project, where he ended up with a non-speaking gig as a mugger who adds to Jack Lemmon's mid-life crisis by stealing his wallet in *The Prisoner of Second Avenue*. Ever the script-writer, when Lemmon's *Schlemiel* fights back, Stallone decided to ad lib, 'Are you nuts?' And why not? His contribution to *The Lords of Flatbush* got him a writing credit and praise from *Time* magazine.

Unfortunately, *The Prisoner of Second Avenue* wasn't written by a couple of unknowns like *The Lords of Flatbush*'s Verona and Davidson. The 1975 film was an adaptation of a hit stage play by the most successful writer in the history of the theatre. After Stallone contributed his three bits, everyone thought he was nuts! Or as the script supervisor whispered to him when the production came to a halt, 'Excuse me, but you can't ad-lib Neil Simon!'

(Twenty years later, another wilful performer, Kim Basinger, would even more egregiously criticise Simon on the set of his film, *The Marrying Man*, complaining about one scene and demanding, 'Get me a writer who can write comedy!')

While Stallone never envied his brother's success, maybe because they struggled in different areas of the entertainment industry, he suffered a real case of career-envy when his *Flatbush* co-stars prospered hugely and he ended up playing a mute mugger. Winkler, King and Blakely all went on to TV superstardom. Stallone was stuck in a bombed-out apartment with only the valiantly typing Sasha and cockroaches for company.

But not for long. He decided to follow his *Flatbush* friends to Hollywood, and his pay from that film provided the funds. Although Stallone had managed to save $4,000, he only spent $40 on a ten-year-old Oldsmobile. The actor with his wife and Butkus, their 110-pound bull mastiff, drove cross county to Hollywood like countless other hopefuls had before and have since, only his fate would be different from the vast majority of these wannabes who eventually became never-wases.

Probably myth-making again, Stallone later claimed the Olds finally blew up at the corner of Sunset and Vine, Hollywood's iconic intersection. The car may have collapsed in the vicinity, however, since he and Sasha ended up renting a one-room apartment for $215 a month a few blocks west of the famous corner, just above another landmark, Mann's Chinese Theatre on Hollywood Boulevard.

Although the location was legendary, the reality was creepy. Despite its historical significance, the area was and remains a blighted stretch of land which millions of dollars of federal and city funds have failed to resuscitate.

Stallone, however, was too busy to notice he had traded a freezing slum apartment on one coast for a sunny slum apartment on another. All his energy was poured into writing, if not *the* Great American Screenplay, certainly one of the greatest and most commercially successful scripts of all time.

# Chapter Four

# Rocking the Boat

Stallone had a new home and a new piece of jewellery on his finger. Sasha still had the typewriter, but she also had a new name and matching jewellery. The same year they moved west, the room-mates of two years decided to formalise their living arrangement with a marriage certificate. Sasha Czach became Sasha Stallone on 28 December 1974. Her new husband became even more obsessed with writing and acting.

Fortunately, if that's the right word, Sasha could now devote all her time to transcribing her husband's scratchings to the type-written page. She finally abandoned her day job as a waitress because Stallone began to find regular if meagre-paying work on TV series like *Kojak* and *Police Story*. However, he found himself maddeningly typecast as thugs in what amounted to bit parts. But at least they kept his wife off the restaurant floor and at home typing. She found plenty of full-time employment there. Stallone's short-lived acting gigs allowed him to spend lots of time on his other passion, writing. Acting at the time wasn't very satisfying, but writing was therapeutic.

He hit the yellow notepads every morning at 6.30 a.m. as dedicated and single-minded with his screenplays as he was at the gym. The dedication finally paid off with his autobiography-flavoured script, *Hell's Kitchen*. Producers John Roach and Ron Suppa paid him what seemed like a fortune at the time – $25,000 – for this tale of three brothers set in the '40s. One brother is an aspiring wrestler. His siblings, one of whom would hopefully be played by Stallone, plan to use their more talented brother as a ticket out of the script's neighbourhood and Stallone's birthplace. The film failed to get made, but the writing fee was a godsend since he earned only $1,400 that year (1975) from playing thugs (again!) in three features, *Capone* (as a really *big* thug, Frank Nitti), *Death Race 2000* and *Farewell, My Lovely*. Stallone was down to his last four dollars, he later claimed, when the Nitti gig saved him from financial meltdown.

Nitti in some ways was an improvement on previous typecasting, since at least in his words the gangster was a 'thinking man's thug'. *Death Race 2000* allowed him to play a thug with wheels. The futuristic thriller, his biggest-budgeted film to date, put him behind the wheels of a racecar in a cross-country contest where the participants earn extra points for running over pedestrians *en route* to the finish line. Like *The Lords of Flatbush*, the film co-starred another actor who would go on to small screen stardom, David Carradine, *Kung Fu*'s future grasshopper. *Death Race 2000* was a commercial hit, but did nothing for Stallone's career or his bank balance, since he didn't have profit participation. That would have to wait for his next film, when profit-sharing would pay off big time.

These roles helped salve the disappointment over other jobs that got away in films like *Dog Day Afternoon*, *Rollerball*, *Serpico* and *The Godfather, Part II*. Stallone seriously considered leaving the business altogether after he got rejected as an extra in *The Godfather* sequel. But his most gnawing rejection at the time came from a film he thought he would be perfect for, considering how much time he spent at the gym. Stallone longed to play the bodybuilder in *Stay Hungry*, but the part went to an actor with even fewer credits but much bigger muscles, somebody called Arnold Schwarzenegger.

Even though it never made it to the screen as originally written, the sale of his *Hell's Kitchen* script encouraged him to keep on scratching while Sasha kept on typing. Sasha became pregnant at this time, and the coming child also provided financial motivation, although desperation might be a better term.

Strangely, though, the greatest motivating force was his mother. Or more accurately, her prediction that success would come as a writer in seven years. Mom had made that astrological prognostication six and a half years earlier. Time was almost up. The baby was due and so was his mother's forecast.

Stallone finally examined his previous writing and discovered what was wrong with all his scripts. They were autobiographical. His life was a downer, and so were all his screenplays. It finally occurred to him that other 'losers' went to the movies to see winners, not variations on their own predicament. That epiphany would translate into a career-making script. But first there was a little inspiration provided by an event that he shouldn't have even been at because the admission price was an extravagance the couple couldn't afford.

15 March 1975 was a pivotal date in Stallone's life. He bought a ticket to a closed-circuit screening of a prizefight. Muhammad Ali fought a grotesquely outclassed pug named Chuck Wepner. Stallone saw the match at the Wiltern Theatre on Wilshire and Western Boulevards in Hollywood on a giant TV screen. The opponents were so mismatched, the fight wasn't sold out. Ali was just there for another multi-million dollar pay day. Wepner's David against Goliath status intrigued Stallone. Stallone's screenplay based on the fight would coin a new term for the phenomenon of underdog, 'Rocky'.

Wepner wasn't even ranked in the Top Ten of heavyweight contenders, and sports writers considered him an even bigger joke because he had delusions he could actually beat Ali, at the time and possibly still considered the greatest fighter in the history of the sport. Jaded journalists thought Wepner, like Ali, was just there a big pay day, although it was nowhere near as much as the champ's. Wepner had other ideas – if not to win, at least to last the entire 15 rounds. At one point in fact, he knocked Ali to the canvas, although some witnesses claimed he had stepped on Ali's foot and pushed rather than knocked him down. Ali won the fight on points, but Wepner remained standing after the final bell. He considered himself a winner, even though he lost. So did Stallone, and thus a film series and an enduring career were born.

'Chuck Wepner – a battling, bruising type of club fighter who had never really made the big time – was now having his shot. He would barely go three rounds, most of the predictions said. Well, he went 15 . . . And he can hold his head up high for ever no matter what happens,' Stallone wrote in a first-person account in *US* magazine.

Legend has it that he sat down and wrote out the first draft of *Rocky* in three days. Reality is a bit more, well, believable. Stallone spent an entire month after the Ali–Wepner fight thinking about the script and especially its hero. Only after that did he sit down in a manic burst and crank out the script. Sasha typed each page as he tore it off his notepad.

'Sasha was called upon to go above and beyond the call of duty. We'd watch the sun go up and the sun go down and we'd eat standing up and she would strugggle and slap herself in the face to keep awake,' he recalled.

Besides Wepner, Stallone had another source of 'inspiration'. He was behind on the rent, and the landlord 'wanted me on the kerb', he said.

The first draft, unfortunately, was a downer and didn't reflect the spirit of Wepner that had captivated Stallone in the first place. The script was simply too autobiographical, reflecting Stallone's poverty, living conditions and his wife's pregnancy, which they could ill afford.

Rocky Balboa took a dive in the original draft! His trainer, Mickey, who eventually would be played as a charming curmudgeon by Burgess Meredith, was a grotesque bigot who screamed racial slurs at Rocky during the fight to get him to hit harder. Instead, Rocky becomes so incensed by Mickey's racism, Stallone says the 'hero . . . lets himself get hit with a punch and then purposely falls flat on his face and loses the fight on a TKO'. Rocky uses the prize money to buy his girlfriend a pet shop. Downer. Bummer.

Even Stallone realised that. When his then agent, Larry Kubik, got him a 'pitch' meeting with an up-and-coming producer named Gene Kirkwood, who worked for A-list producers Irwin Winkler and Robert Chartoff, Stallone didn't even bring up *Rocky*. Instead, he pitched a script he'd written about a cabdriver who decides to run for mayor of Philadelphia.

Kirkwood thought the concept amusing but lacking in energy. He asked if the young writer-actor had any other ideas. Stallone hesitated. Rocky was still gestating, an embryonic character nowhere near delivery. He told Kirkwood the storyline. The producer liked the idea but pounced on its biggest flaw: the hero takes a dive.

Kirkwood sent him back to his flat with orders to write a second draft. With both the writer and his typist popping caffeine pills, they turned out a new script in 86 hours. The producer liked the revised script, then collaborated with his protégé on a third draft during the summer of 1975. Stallone went overboard on Kirkwood's suggestion to make the script more upbeat and actually wrote an ending in which the outclassed pug beats the heavyweight champion. Kirkwood reined in his co-writer's new found optimism and settled for Rocky, like Wepner, going the full 15 rounds.

Kirkwood showed his bosses the new script. Chartoff and Winkler, who helped Jane Fonda win her first Oscar nomination with *They Shoot Horses, Don't They?*, loved the character-driven drama and took the project to United Artists, which like every other studio in town, was looking for vehicles for the huge crop of handsome leading men and charismatic character actors turned leads who dominated the screen at the time. Possible 'Rockys' on the short list included Ryan O'Neal, Burt Reynolds, Robert Redford and James Caan. On a longer, less likely list: Gene Hackman, Jack Nicholson and Paul Newman.

UA offered Stallone $75,000 for the script, manna from heaven considering his wife's condition and their imminent new home on the kerb outside the apartment building. Stallone did a very Rocky-like thing. He bucked the odds and turned the offer down. He had not only written *Rocky*, he *was* Rocky. 'The story was about not selling out, about having faith in yourself, about going the distance as a million-to-one shot,' he said.

UA thought this was just a negotiating ploy on the part of his seasoned agent, Kubik, and upped the offer to $125,000.

Thinking about this fortune, Stallone said, 'gave me a monumental headache', but the pain of selling out hurt even more.

Every man, the cliché goes, has his price. UA thought it might be about $350,000, which was the final amount the studio offered Stallone to bow out and let a major star step into the ring.

It was crisis time in the Stallone household, uh, tenement. Sasha and Sylvester were stilling living in their $215-a-month rat-trap. The baby was due in a few months. Stallone himself felt he'd rather bury the script in the backyard than let another actor steal perhaps his only shot at movie stardom. But he also felt compelled to get Sasha's OK. Much like Adrian, his girlfriend in *Rocky*, Sasha stood in his corner and told him to keep swinging. And turn down $350,000. They were a perfect match. A quixotic pair in hindsight. At the time, they probably felt they were both nuts.

Sasha asked her husband what that amount of money 'looked like'. He said he had no idea, since they were down to their last $106 in the bank. That settled the matter, Sasha said wisely in retrospect, insanely at the time: 'I don't know either, so I guess I wouldn't really miss it.'

Stallone asked his pregnant wife, 'But if I don't sell it, how do you feel about having to go into the backyard and eat grass?' In a reply Stallone should have plagiarised for the next draft of his screenplay, Sasha said, 'I'd sooner move to a trailer in the middle of a swamp than for you to sell *Rocky*!'

Stallone later echoed his wife's explanation: 'If you've never seen that kind of money, you don't miss it.' He told the producers to tell the studio the script was not for sale at any price – even a million bucks – unless he got to star. His conviction was ultimately contagious. Kirkwood's initial reaction was less bullish. 'Kid, why don't you take up sky-diving without a parachute?' he asked him. Chartoff and Winkler warned him that his intransigence might kill the project, but they made a counter-offer to UA. They would shoot the film on a shoestring budget of $1.75 million with the screenwriter as star.

United Artists made a counter-offer themselves. The producers could cast Francis the Talking Horse if they liked, but they would only get $1 million to make the movie.

The studio tacked on three other conditions. Stallone would go quietly after the first 30 days of shooting if the dailies (footage screened for technical mistakes at the end of each day) looked awful. The producers would have to put up their own money if the film went over its million-dollar budget. (Chartoff and Winkler ended up mortgaging their homes to pay for the completion bond, a form of insurance if the production self-destructed.) And a piddling matter which Stallone passive-aggressively ignored – the egomaniacal Muhammad Ali character would have to be turned into a Jamaican so fans of the champ wouldn't tear out the theatre seats.

A little sweetener, however, was added to these bitter demands. Apparently, the studio didn't have great expectations for the B-movie's box-office prospects and agreed to give Stallone a percentage of the profits.

Stallone and the producers sat down together and pared the budget to the bone. Instead of taking $350,000 for the script, he gladly settled for 20 grand. His salary as star would be SAG (Screen Actors Guild) minimum, called scale. Stallone accepted everything. As he later said, 'I would have settled for $1.10 a day and a hot lunch!'

Other economies were fun. To save money on the rest of the cast's salary, his father got the job as bell-ringer in the climactic fight. His brother sang one of his own compositions on a streetcorner in another scene. Even the family's bull mastiff, Butkus, earned his SAG card by playing Rocky's pet, a case of typecasting if ever there was one. Sasha, who was just embarking on a successful career as a photographer, agreed to shoot the publicity stills on the set for the press kit and advertising campaign.

The tight budget meant a tight shooting schedule, a back-breaking 28 days, the time more typically alloted a TV-movie, and about as long as it took to write the first draft.

The choice of director was a strange one. John Avildsen specialised in downbeat films like 1970's *Joe*, in which a right-wing hardhat goes berserk and kills his hippie daughter, and *Save the Tiger*, in which an insolvent clothing manufacturer burns down his factory for the insurance money. On the other hand, *Save the Tiger* did win its star, Jack Lemmon, an Oscar in 1973, but the director's thematic preoccupations seemed 180 degrees away from *Rocky*'s upbeat, fairytale quality.

Avildsen did have one thing going for him the cash-strapped filmmakers liked. The director preferred to work cheap. Avildsen had allegedly volunteered to reduce the budget on a previous film because he hated extravagance. The filmmaker's frugality even extended to his own asking fee, which he cut to $50,000 after falling in love with the script. Wisely, like his star, he also accepted a cut of the profits which wiser heads didn't think would ever come.

Maybe the change in his career brightened Stallone's mood because he rewrote the script one more time before principal photography began. Any cynicism displayed by the original Rocky, who was willing to take a fall, fell by the wayside. The new, improved pug was sweetness incarnate. Also, much dumber than Stallone's original, jaded incarnation. 'I see him with a man's body and the mind of a 15-year-old. Not smart. He's sentimental and vulnerable, easily hurt. He doesn't dig books but he can relate to people,' said the writer who once dismissed Flaubert for failing to write a bestseller.

Reflecting Sasha's unconditional support amid the prospect of financial ruin, Stallone also ennobled his screen girlfriend, Adrian. She became a selfless soulmate who supported her man unconditionally. Only in the movies! And the Stallones' rat-trap off Hollywood Boulevard.

Avildsen's participation and word of mouth about the script attracted two 'name' actors who normally wouldn't have considered appearing in such a low-budget film with a no-name star. In fact, two recent Oscar nominees were attracted like moths to the heat of Stallone's script. The same year *Rocky* went into production, Burgess Meredith won a best supporting Oscar nomination for *The Day of the Locust*. Meredith signed on as Mickey, by now cleansed of any racism and as noble as Stallone had made the new Rocky. Nobody was going to take a fall in this film.

An even bigger catch was Talia Shire, Yale film school graduate, sister of director Francis Ford Coppola, and a year

ABOVE: Stallone at Manor High School, a private institution for troubled youths, where he was known as Michael (Seth Poppel)

RIGHT: Stallone's mother claimed her son failed to make the football team because of poor grades, but this yearbook photo shows Stallone (*front row, third from left*) on the team (Seth Poppel)

Stallone and his beautiful first wife, Sasha Czack, were married for eleven years. When they divorced in 1985, Sasha collected a $32-million settlement (Photofest)

*The Lords of Flatbush* (1974) was Stallone's first big film, but it would be another two years before *Rocky* made him a superstar (Photofest)

Stallone wrote this scene with Maria Smith, who played his girlfriend in *The Lords of Flatbush*, and received a writing credit and praise from *Time* magazine for his efforts (Photofest)

A year before *Rocky*, Stallone had a small role as gangster Frank Nitti in *Capone* (1975) (Everett Collection)

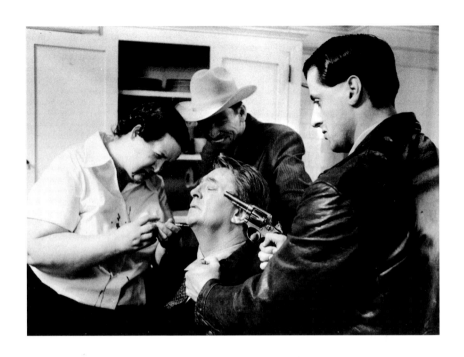

Stallone was often typecast as a thug or gangster before *Rocky* made him a lovable hero; (*above*) in *Farewell, My Lovely* (1975) and (*below*) in *Cannonball* (1976)
(Everett Collection)

ABOVE: Stallone co-wrote and directed *Staying Alive* (1983) which revived
John Travolta's career (Photofest)

BELOW: Dolly Parton tries to turn cab-driver Stallone into a country and western singer
in *Rhinestone* (1984) (Everett Collection)

*Vanity Fair* called Stallone's second wife the 'freakishly beautiful' Brigitte Nielson. Everyone else called the Danish model 'gorgeous' (Photofest)

ABOVE: Stallone in 1982's *First Blood*, which launched the enormously successful *Rambo* film series (Photofest)

RIGHT: In *Rambo*, Stallone's muscles apparently attracted female fans, who comprised 40 per cent of his audience, and helped make the film his biggest hit (Photofest)

Stallone received a record-breaking $12 million to arm wrestle in *Over the Top* (1987) (Everett Collection)

earlier an Oscar nominee for her Mafia widow in *The Godfather* sequel. The script was so hot, Shire had to audition for the role of Adrian, but she was willing to accept this minor humiliation. Her only success had been in two films directed by her brother. She wanted to escape Francis's orbit and typecasting as Connie Corleone. She got the job and slashed her fee to $7,500.

Other crucial casting included lesser knowns who would become famous because of *Rocky*. Former Oakland Raiders football star Carl Weathers signed as the Ali-clone, who by now was no longer Jamaican and just as loud-mouthed as his real-life inspiration.

The original meeting between Stallone and Weathers did not go well. As part of the audition, Stallone asked the huge football player who was four inches taller at six feet two and a year younger (28) to go a few rounds with him. During the match, Weathers' enthusiasm overwhelmed him and he hit Stallone full in the face. The star didn't throw a tantrum, but reminded Weathers, 'Hey, this is only an audition.'

Weathers thought he was sparring with the screenwriter and suggested that the star of the film step into the ring, since he'd be a better-matched opponent. Stallone wasn't offended and said, smiling, 'I *am* the actor.' Weathers's feistiness charmed Stallone, despite the sore jaw, and convinced him he was right for the role of the contentious Ali-alike.

Burt Young came aboard as Adrian's brother and Rocky's best friend. Young's Paulie was possibly even more intellectually challenged than his pug pal.

As part of his 'personal pre-production', Stallone decided to transform his body to suit the role once again. During the interminable *The Lords of Flatbush* shoot, he binged on ice cream for two years to create the thuggish Stanley Rosiello. Rocky needed a different look since he was an athlete whose body had to look like one that could go the distance and remain standing after 15 rounds, not collapse in a puddle of fat, which Stanley probably would have done in a match up with Apollo Creed. As he would in so many later films, Stallone tailored his diet not only to fit his character but to alter his brain chemistry so that the man and role would merge. Stallone has always rejected the term Method actor. *His* Method is methodical dieting. For *Rocky*, he ate only protein and no carbohydrates.

It's fortunate that the shoot lasted less than a month because a prolonged diet like that can cause major health problems. Maybe the actor was tapping early memories of rickets from a vitamin deficiency caused by his parents' poverty. Or maybe he was just obsessed with making his film and role the best possible. For whatever reasons, the all-meat-no-potatoes actually altered his way of thinking and speaking, he claimed. The lack of energy provided by carbohydrates slowed his mental reactions and slurred his speech – as if he needed any help.

The regimen, he said, 'severely changed my intelligence level. I went on a strict shrimp and shellfish diet, with no carbohydrates whatsoever, and eventually my intelligence level dropped to the point where I'd want to listen to country and western music, which is really bizarre for me.' (So it was shellfish that persuaded him to play a singing cowboy in *Rhinestone* eight years later!)

Before and during shooting, he lived the life of a boxer training for a big fight, which he was – the fight of his career. Although pressed for time, Stallone increased the length of his workout, a cross-training compulsion of weight-lifting, jogging, shadow-boxing, and jumping rope.

Sasha didn't complain when he brought his work home with him, setting up a punching bag in the middle of the already crowded apartment. Despite the 20 grand he received for the script and his acting fee, Stallone was so consumed with making the film he didn't have the time or energy to move out of the hellhole above Hollywood Boulevard. After a high protein dinner of shrimp, Stallone was wired and would spend the rest of the evening pirouetting around the bag. To get her husband to stop, Sasha claimed she would ring the oven bell and scream, '"Time!" I went through horrors. He trained as if he really were preparing for a championship.'

For four months prior to filming, Stallone and Weathers worked out together. After the gym, they collaborated on rewriting the climactic fight scene. In the pre-shooting script, Stallone joked that he had simply written '14 pages of left, right, right, left, left hook'. The co-stars tried moves out in the ring, then blocked them on paper. They studied the classic fights of champs known for their balletic style – Joe Louis, Rocky Marciano, Sonny Liston and, of course, Muhammad Ali. Avildsen shot this work in progress on Super 8mm film, and the trio critiqued the primitive 'dailies' to decide which moves would work best on the big screen in 35mm.

Complicating things was the fact that both men abandoned safety for realism. They tried to pull their punches, but more often than not, although the whack you hear on the screen may be enhanced with sound effects, the collision is real. Stallone joked long after the film wrapped, 'My neck is still stiff after months of snapping back from those jabs of Carl Weathers. He got so fast that when I was editing the film I'd find a punch in just one frame. There are 24 frames a second, so that was 1/24th of a second and the punch was gone.'

Finally, the film was ready to start shooting on location in Philadelphia on 9 January 1976.

The temperature was 19°F that day and Stallone said he had never felt so cold in his life, although the weather was only a contributing factor to his body temperature. He was scared, he told Sasha in the trailer *en route* to the location. 'On the ride over, I discovered more about myself than I had in the past nine or ten years. I had gone over every scene in my mind, every piece of dialogue, every bit of business. I knew it was under control. But a great wave of responsibility came over me. I knew that if I failed, the movie would fail.'

Then he asked his wife and crew members to leave the trailer. Stallone looked in the mirror and said to himself, 'Sylvester, 29 years you've been talking a great game. Now either you prove it, or you're dead.' I knew when I looked in that mirror that this man was either going to walk out a hero or a totally disgraced wretch who had been living a life of illusions – sad, gas-filled dreams.'

When he looked in the mirror, he saw Rocky, not Sylvester. It helped that he wore makeup that gave him a fake scarred eye, a stocking cap and a filthy sweat suit with 'Italian Stallion' scrawled on the back in grease pencil. Even so, doubts about his ability to become Rocky lingered. 'I still wasn't certain I could do it until there was a knock at the door and the assistant director said, 'OK, Sly, we're ready!'

'I turned around and said, "Sly went back to California. He told me to take his place. Yeah, the name's Rocky, how ya doin"?' The AD replied, "You're on, Rock."'

The assistant confirmed what Stallone already knew after his pep talk in front of the mirror. 'When I walked out of the trailer and my foot hit the pavement and the cold tightened my face, it was in the bag.'

\* \* \*

Because of carefully planned pre-production to cut costs, the month-long shoot went smoothly – technically if not emotionally.

The board of health closed the commissary, which was a mess since the tiny budget didn't allow for a professional caterer. Some of the actors complained about their shabby accommodations on the set, more like 'stalls', Talia Shire said, 'than trailers'.

Although it didn't slow down production, Stallone's self-admitted obsession with details antagonised everyone from lowly grips to the director himself. Avildsen admitted that the crew hated Stallone 'intensely', but the director attributed at least some of the enmity to the star's acting ability, his knack for getting the crew – and later millions of filmgoers world wide – to think he actually was Rocky. 'It was very strange,' Avildsen said. '[The crew] really thought that Sly was a beat-up club fighter. They just couldn't get through their minds that they were watching a helluva great actor. We tried to get them to watch the daily rushes, but they just turned away.'

A micro-manager, Stallone had an opinion on everything, from what kinds of eyewear and hairdo the mousy Adrian should wear as her character gradually becomes more assertive to disagreements with Burgess Meredith over the length of fight scenes. The star conceded he managed to make enemies of just about everyone on the set. Some crew members demanded their names be taken off the credits, a curious example of cutting off one's nose to spite one's face since a credit on a huge hit is invaluable for future employment.

Co-star Burt Young defended Stallone's prickly behaviour and attributed it to wearing too many hats: actor, writer, fight co-ordinator, 'fashion consultant' for Adrian. 'That kid, Sylvester, he was *tough*. [But] it's a hard thing to walk into a film where it's on your back like that. And the son of a gun fooled me! I have nothing but respect for the kid,' said Young, who would show his respect by repeating his role in sequels.

Then there was dad, Frank Sr. He neglected his bell-ringing duties for reasons best left to discussions between his son and his therapist. The elder Stallone would allow Weathers to keep slugging his son long after the segment should have ended. Stallone remembers hissing through his teeth at his father, 'The bell! The bell!' while Weathers pounded away, waiting for the cue to stop the assault. The only break in fighting came when filming had to pause while makeup men applied more fake cuts and bruises to the real ones Stallone had already suffered.

The combined attentiveness of Weathers's punches and Stallone Sr's inattentiveness with the bell resulted in some nasty injuries to the star. Their first on-screen fight, shot at the Los Angeles Sports Arena, left Stallone with a cracked hip bone. Jogging on Philadelphia's mean – and hard concrete – streets resulted in a pulled tendon. 'They had to take me home in a wheelbarrow,' Stallone said.

Clashes continued during post-production. Stallone, of course, sat in on the editing, and the tiny room filled with colliding egos. In one argument over whether a scene should be cut, *Newsweek* magazine said that the beefy actor picked up the diminutive director and threw him up against the door.

The biggest fight at the movieola involved the ending. Both the star and director agreed Rocky would technically lose the match. His personal victory was going the distance. There were many ways to win, Stallone believed, and he wanted the film's ending to reflect that. But in Avildsen's version, it was unclear that Apollo Creed had actually won. Stallone fought to make that clear and won that fight.

The director admitted doing battle with his star, but it was a fight for a good cause, a great movie. When they weren't shoving each other, the close, in-your-face collaboration worked magnificently.

'We were able to shape the story, to bring out things just because the actor and the writer were there on the scene in one person, someone who understood what a scene needed. We were able to bounce ideas off one another,' Avildsen said. That is, when the actor-writer wasn't bouncing the director off the wall! 'And Stallone showed himself to have a deep sensitivity for the part he was playing.'

Even when they disagreed, Avildsen never found Stallone's demands arbitrary or the wilfulness of a self-absorbed star. Both men shared the same mission. To make the film as good as it could be. 'I have never found the hustler instinct in Sylvester,' Avildsen said. 'During the entire experience of *Rocky* he was exceptionally enthusiastic, even naïve. He was terrific to work with – he had no pride of authorship. Everything was for the good of the project. And he knew everyone's lines because he had written the script. He faced everything with a smile on his face. At least that was when I worked with him. Before he was a star.'

Avildsen's last statement, made a few years after *Rocky* did indeed turn its creator into a star, implies volumes of what happened to the once ego-less, collaborative actor. A hint just how much Stallone changed post-*Rocky* comes from Avildsen's refusal to direct *Rocky III*, although he still had enough fondness for his ex-collaborator to urge Stallone to direct the second sequel and return himself as director of number five.

Both men agreed that the ending of the first *Rocky* lacked something and reshot the finale, bringing Adrian back into the picture. In the original cut, Rocky left the ring alone. In the now famous fairy tale ending, Adrian throws her arms around the 'loser' and screams, 'I love you, Rocky!'

Another 'production' came to fruition during post-production, Stallone and Sasha's baby boy, who was born in May 1976. The actor shocked interviewers by saying the birth had been astrologically planned so the child would be born a

Taurus. Sasha, he said, willed herself to give birth between 10 a.m. and noon that day when the position of the planets was exactly right. The child's name was chosen with equal care. Sage Moonblood. The first name for wisdom, the second in honour of one of Stallone's favourite Edgar Allan Poe works.

Long before the movie came out in November 1976, the grapevine became garrulous that United Artists had not just a sleeper hit but a blockbuster on its hands. Stallone fuelled the hype, which turned out to be an underestimate, by predicting the movie would gross $100 million.

A class at the University of Southern California ultraprestigious film school, the home of George Lucas, applauded during a private screening. *Rocky* also became the hottest ticket on the 'Bel Air circuit', private screenings in the homes of studio execs and producers, where careers are made and destroyed. Excited word filtered down from the Mount Olympus of Bel Air and the Hollywood Hills to the public. As expectations grew pre-release, UA opened up its previously tight wallet and paid for a massive advertising campaign.

Stallone treated his mother to a private screening of the film at the studio. Her astrological prediction had come true. The film unspooling in front of her in the dark confirmed it. Sounding like a healthier version of Jimmy Cagney's Oedipal-hexed hood screaming, 'Top of the world, Ma! Top of the world!' in *White Heat*, Stallone leapt up on stage early during the screening and shouted, 'Hey, Ma, I made it, I made it, Ma!' Jacqueline cried.

*Rocky* arrived in theatres with seemingly impossible expectations, which it quickly met and exceeded. Its opening weekend of $14 million surpassed everyone's hopes except perhaps *Rocky*'s self-confident *auteur*. The Cinema II in Manhattan, where it premiered, took in $40,000 during its first three days of release.

The *New York Times*'s Vincent Canby voiced a minority opinion, labelling the film over-hyped and underwhelming. 'Not since *The Great Gatsby* two years ago has any film come into town more absurdly oversold than *Rocky*, the sentimental little slum movie.' The film, he added, was 'pure Hollywood make-believe of the 1930's . . . Mr Stallone's Rocky is less a performance than an impersonation . . . it's a studied routine, not a character.'

Other reviewers loved *Rocky* and the actor who embodied him. The New York *Daily News*'s Kathleen Carroll gave it four stars and said, '*Rocky* is a glowing tribute to the human spirit. Stallone is a totally engaging Rocky, playing him with a mixture of boyish intensity, lusty sensuality, and cheerful innocence.'

The most famous critic of the era and a celebrity in her own right, Judith Crist of *The Saturday Review*, put herself firmly in Balboa's corner. '*Rocky* is a delightful human comedy . . . a latter-day Marty in its romantic story of two "losers" . . . A deeply personal film written out of a picaresque youth by Sylvester Stallone . . . a sincere, rousing little film that raises the spirits and gladdens the heart.'

*New York* magazine called it a 'pugnacious, charming, grimy, beautiful fairy tale. It is a small pearl of realism.' *Newsweek* seemed to love the actor even more than the film: 'He's the first leading man to come along that's a *man* and yet he's still like a gentle little kitten in the film . . . Innocently sexy, his acting is unaffected and he conveys deep vulnerability but without baroque psychological nuances.'

Another 'critic' whose rave wasn't exactly disinterested, United Artists chief Mike Medavoy crowed, 'I can't recall such excitement about a new movie and a new star since maybe *Giant* and James Dean.'

The public loved the movie even more than the critics did. The final US and Canadian gross totalled a whopping $117 million, a record-breaking hundred to one return on the initial investment. United Artists had hoped to make a million or two dollars profit. The studio's take amounted to $55 million.

In return for cutting his screenwriting fee and working as an actor for union minimum, Stallone received one per cent of the film's profits for the script and two per cent for his performance. A year later, as *Rocky* continued to break records, Stallone had yet to see any of his profit participation from the studio. 'It's lost in transit,' he said bitterly, with only the original $25,000 acting-writing payment to show for his efforts. United Artists heard about his displeasure in a magazine interview, which included the threat of a lawsuit by the star. The day after the article appeared, Stallone's agent pulled a publicity stunt by delivering $2 million in cash via armoured truck to the set of his client's new film.

With this dramatic windfall, he mothballed the ten-year-old Oldsmobile that had conveyed the Stallones cross country and bought a top of the line white Mercedes SE with leather upholstery. To paraphrase Fitzgerald, 'The *nouveaux riches* are different from you and me!'

Stallone and his movie had charmed the critics and compelled the ticket-buying public to part with lots of its money. The only institution left to pay its respects to Stallone's accomplishments was the Academy of Motion Picture Arts and Sciences, and at Oscar time, respect was indeed paid. Nominated for both best actor and best screenplay, Stallone found himself in rarefied company. Only Charlie Chaplin and Orson Welles had pulled off a double-header like that before.

The Oscar ceremony itself must have created mixed feelings for the newly minted superstar. The film cleaned up in every category, it seemed, except the ones in which Stallone was personally nominated. John Avildsen won for best director. *Rocky*'s producers Irwin Winkler and Robert Chartoff proudly went to the podium when the award for best picture of 1976 was announced. The film also took home a statuette for best editing. But Stallone got shut out of the best actor and screenplay categories. Peter Finch was a no-show to accept the best actor award for *Network* since he had died two months prior to the ceremony on 29 March 1977. Finch's Oscar was the first best actor award to be given posthumously. You can almost imagine Rocky Balboa – if not Stallone – saying dimly to himself at the Dorothy Chandler Pavilion, 'Beat out by a corpse!' Similarly, *Rocky*'s script was no match for *Network*'s, written by one of the great playwrights of the twentieth century, Paddy Chayefsky, who KO'ed Stallone for best original screenplay. Stallone couldn't take grim satisfaction in the fact that his leading lady was similarly shut out by Faye Dunaway's predatory TV executive in *Network*. He genuinely liked Talia

Shire, his on-screen girlfriend, and her loss couldn't mollify his. Generously, when Winkler and Chartoff ran on stage to pick up the best picture Oscar, they kept waving at the star in the audience until he sheepishly joined them at the podium, even though Stallone did not have a producer's credit on the film.

The Oscars were a disappointment. But other awards and the Olympian universe of a superstar would take the sting out of the Oscar snub. Later in 1977, he received recognition for what *really* counts in an art form that is, after all, called the film *business*, not the film *arts*. The National Association of Theatre Owners named him Male Star of the year. The 8,000-member claque honoured him for *Rocky*'s box-office performance, but the award also represented future good fortune. The operators of first-run theatres decide well in advance of word of mouth, reviews or even sneak previews which films to book in their movie houses. NATO's nod meant that whatever Stallone offered them next, he was a guaranteed booking around the country.

*Rocky* had made him rich (at least after he threatened legal action to collect his three per cent cut) and adulated world-wide. It had given him new wheels and soon a palatial mansion in the very best neighbourhood in Beverly Hills. Shortly before Sage's birth in May 1976, Sly and Sasha decamped to a four-bedroom mansion only a few miles geographically, but socio-economically light years away from Hollywood Boulevard. Their new home was located in Coldwater Canyon, the chateaubriand of the filet mignon that is Beverly Hills. Previously owned by comedian Ernie Kovacs, the home had whimsical furnishings. The circular driveway leading up to the house rested on a giant turntable which automatically transported guests' cars to the proper parking space. A wine cellar had fake cobwebs and a stuffed rhinoceros head spouted water from its snout in a fountain near the entrance.

However, in a classic case of be careful what you wish for because it may come true, Stallone found himself living his fondest fantasy while he also asked himself the question posed by Peggy Lee in the classic song, 'Is That All There Is?' The vermin-infested apartment was gone. The new baby had plenty to eat. Even Butkus, the overweight bull mastiff, whom Stallone had almost dumped at the pound because he couldn't afford to feed the 110-pound dog, trotted alongside the Stallone Gravy Train.

Stallone began to misbehave. Not horrifically in a Sean Penn/Robert Downey Jr sort of way. The police were never called and Stallone never got busted for drugs or spousal battery. But success, he discovered, as so many before him had, was no panacea. With or without an Oscar, the mansion, the money, the public adulation, you first have to *like* yourself. At this time, buried memories of criticism from parents and peers had Stallone asking himself, 'Why do you like me *now?*' Or as he confessed to one writer before the full impact of *Rocky* had turned his humility into self-confidence, 'I've never considered myself intelligent; I've considered myself clever. I have the gift of taking the negative and making it into a positive.' Yet, on other occasions, he would claim an IQ of 139, one point below genius.

The enormity of his disenchantment can be heard in self-posed questions like this: 'It's funny, but now there's this great herd of people who are coming forth and saying, "I like you!" It happened to Rocky too. I feel like saying to them, "Where were you when I was living in Hotel Barf, eating hot and cold running disease?" They say, "Oh, we were holding it back, Sly, because we didn't want you to get a swelled head."'

# Chapter Five

# Post-Euphoria Depression

Journalists, especially those who had their own unproduced screenplays growing mould on the shelf, seemed to resent Stallone's claim that *Rocky* had been written in three days. Some of them had been trying to get out of the low-paid world of print journalism for years, and here was this college dropout making stardom seem like a three-day wonder.

Stallone loved to boast about his prolificness. A more self-effacing superstar would have mentioned in interviews that only the first draft of *Rocky* had been scratched out so fast. The writer had had to do several humbling rewrites. But humility was not the word used to describe him in the press at the time. One magazine wrote, 'He found he had become an object of contempt.'

Envy turned to derision when he publicised his mother's astrological prediction that success would come in seven years. His belief in his star based on Mom's belief in the stars led many pundits to suspect he was as dim-witted as his monosyllabic screen character. It never occurred to them, perhaps, that Rocky could never have written *Rocky*.

Stallone must have felt as though he was back under his father's wing and those career counsellors who had recommended elevator repair instead of showbiz. He had done such a good job creating Rocky first on paper then on screen, he became identified with the role. People assumed he was stupid.

'People think I've got the IQ of a hockey score,' he said. 'I'm supposed to be this primordial being who slurs his way through life. I've been called a master of the malapropism. What crap! My vocabulary is larger than 90 per cent of the writers I've met.'

Stallone overcompensated on talk shows and in interviews. Balboa was a bimbo; Stallone wanted to demonstrate he was Noel Coward with 16-inch biceps. 'I went out of my way to be overly cute, overly coy, overly outrageous, a real iconoclast, rebellious to the end, to show I'm not Rocky. I'm far more clever, far more complex, far more sexual.

'And in doing that, it shocked people and turned them off. People say, "All right, we've seen enough of it, take your lunch and leave," and the next man moves in. I've seen it happen with my peers. I've seen it happen with so many athletic idols. I have a clipping service, shopping bags full of clips from Australia and New Zealand even, and I am astounded at the anger people have for me.'

It wasn't his 'cuteness' that caused the resentment of the public. Stallone appeared on talk shows and cracked vulgar jokes one magazine said even 'Rocky wouldn't tell in the locker room'. For one TV appearance, he wore a white canvas suit embroidered with a floral pattern – inappropriate wardrobe for the lovable lug the public had fallen in love with. On the same show, he also sang the Sinatra classic, 'My Way'.

Comparisons to Orson Welles and Charlie Chaplin haunted him. He wanted Chaplin's not Welles's career. He didn't want to be a one-hit wonder, chasing the rest of his life for a second *Citizen Kane*. Chaplin represented the ideal, returning in glory to the Oscars in his eighties, honoured for a lifetime of achievement, not forgotten after Rocky.

Typecasting began immediately. Offers to play gangsters predominated. Stallone must have turned them down with a mixture of amusement and frustration. He had almost left the business after failing to find work as an extra on *The Godfather II*. Now, he was being asked to play *capo di tutti capi*. He said *mille grazie* but no thanks.

Rocky Balboa had been conceived as Everyman, perhaps

even Everyloser who transcends his limitations to succeed on his own terms and by his own definition of what success means. The public, however, turned Rocky into Superman as part of its own wish-fulfilment fantasy. It was a fantasy the studios happily bought into.

In fact, one of the first roles offered Stallone in the euphoria of *Rocky*'s popularity was Superman! Showing a career insight that would sadly desert him in later years, Stallone turned down the role that made Christopher Reeve a contenduh. The offer to play the Man of Steel must have been particularly sweet, since the last time he had dressed up as Superboy, in grade school, all he got was public humiliation.

But he showed good taste, not fickleness in his rejection of Superman and other films that didn't measure up to his exacting standards. It was '*déjà vu* all over again', or as he described the tripe served up to him: 'Gangster movies or more fight films, real lame stuff.' Just as he had tested himself with *Rocky*, the actor wanted to continue the artistic challenge. He looked for 'a real test of acting, something that would be kind of important'. Stallone wanted fans and the critics to concede, 'Yeah, all right, he's not a boxer, he can act a little.'

Like his acting career, Sylvester Stallone the screenwriter was hot – perhaps too hot. After writing so many screenplays that were laughed out of pitch meetings – when he could get one – Stallone loved the fact that suddenly anything he put on paper generated heat! An old script of his, *The Bodyguard*, became the project every studio wanted to make after passing on it pre-*Rocky*. The plot reflects the depressive outlook of his starving artist days, but eerily anticipates the plots of future *Rambo*s. In the title role, Stallone would play a man hired to protect the wife and child of an industrialist. The bodyguard screws up and his charges are murdered. The bodyguard turns into, well, Rambo, and goes on a one-man killing spree. Universal snapped up the screenplay for $200,000 with the proviso that the screenwriter also star, a nice change from the days when the studios courted the author of *Rocky* but rejected the man who insisted on playing him. Reflecting his new huge clout, Stallone had it written into the contract that he would get to keep the

Porsche Turbo Carrera used in the film after it wrapped. At this point, any studio in town would have given him a fleet of Porsches for his writing and acting services.

\* \* \*

A little known fact is that nearly every successful film – and even some flops – get hit with a plagiarism lawsuit by a screenwriter who claims a hit was based, at least in part, on his script. Rocky was no exception. Except Stallone found himself in the ironic position of being sued for plagiarising himself.

His earlier script, *Hell's Kitchen*, had been purchased by producers John Roach and Ron Suppa. They claimed Stallone had lifted a Rocky-like character out of *Hell's Kitchen*. They also pointed out that in one draft the boxer was even nicknamed the 'Italian Stallion'. Never mind that in the final draft, also written by Stallone, the boxer had become a wrestler, and unlike Rocky, set in present-day Philadelphia, *Hell's Kitchen* was set in '40s New York.

Stallone seemed alternately amused and angered by the lawsuit, which claimed *Rocky* and *Hell's Kitchen* shared 'theme, mood, format, characters, and structure'. Stallone responded, 'How can it be plagiarism? They're both my scripts. You know, you don't meet a guy in an alley anymore. Now it's, "My lawyer will notify you. I'll meet you in court."'

Wannabe producers weren't the only ones who wanted a piece of him. Paparazzi also wanted a shot. And fans literally seemed to want a piece of him. Stallone complained that when he went to pick up the newspaper on the front porch, 30 photographers would jump out to shoot him. Fans identified too closely with Rocky's toughness and used the star as a personal punching bag. Men didn't shake his hand. They punched him – affectionately, they thought.

For a young man who had tried to draw attention to himself from childhood, the new scrutiny was initially intoxicating but quickly became irritating. 'At first the crowds were fun. I signed a lot of autographs [but] people want more than you can give them. At first they want to touch. Then they want to grab. I'm not a person anymore; I'm someone to be challenged and taunted.'

This was the beginning of the Stallone 'entourage', a creepy assortment of guys in suits who look like linebackers but are there to protect him from smash-and-grab fans. No one punches Stallone anymore, unless they're on a soundstage and a camera is rolling.

*There were fans*: 'It's the strangest thing. I'm signing autographs and this young girl is reaching out to touch me, and she has the most frightening look on her face, as if this instant is transcendent for her. She isn't touching me; she's touching Rocky, an unreal person.'

*And then there were fans from hell*, the kind who on other occasions gun down John Lennon or Gianni Versace. One woman punched him full in the face, and it wasn't to get his attention for an autograph. 'I asked her why she'd done a thing like that, and she said, "Because you got what I want!"'

Stallone's reaction to such assaults recalls Henry Kissinger's famous observation that even paranoid people have enemies. He said, 'One of these days some nutso might have a knife. I'm getting paranoid. As soon as they touch me, my hand balls up into a fist.'

Or touch his car. After being rear-ended by a vehicle, Stallone demanded an apology from the driver, who told him to go to hell. Stallone yelled at the man that his son could have been in the car. The driver repeated the same directions to hell. Stallone then slugged the guy, who eventually received $15,000 in an out-of-court settlement.

The new star distanced himself more and more from a mercurial public that included adoring fans and someone he feared might have a copy of *Catcher in the Rye* and a semi-automatic tucked in his backpocket. The family moved from Coldwater Canyon in Beverly Hills to the slightly more downscale Pacific Palisades nearby. The new home was fortified against intruders with a brick wall. An armed guard stood inside the entrance, and seven closed-circuit TVs with a 360-degree view of the property spied on anyone who approached the sprawling grounds.

The alienation wasn't only from the public. Sasha found herself growing apart from her husband. They had been physically and emotionally close during their crowded apartment days, when he wrote and she typed endless scripts. Sasha was out of a job.

To take some ammo away from the *Hell's Kitchen* plagiarism suit, Stallone retitled it *Paradise Alley*, turned the boxer into a wrestler, and firmly located it in New York's Lower Eastside post-World War II.

Universal put the project into pre-production and gave Stallone a sumptuous office on the lot to make his revisions. Sasha felt abandoned. 'All my ambition, all my energy, went into working with him. The baby and *Rocky* changed that. I was at home with the baby; he was at the studio . . . We were apart for the first time. He'd come home and try to share his day with me, but it was hard for both of us,' she said.

Sasha went so far as to try to share his space when he relocated to Universal. She volunteered to resume her old duties as typist and accompany him to the back lot. He told her to stay home. 'Not being involved made me very, very restless,' Sasha said. 'I started asking if I could come to the studio, but he just said it was boring there. I would say, "Why don't we just be bored together like we used to be?"'

Her husband shut her out of his professional life more and more. After an exciting day on the set, he would 'come home, eat dinner, and fall asleep without saying more than four words', she recalled.

Suddenly, Stallone turned into a traditional, unliberated husband. During his starving actor period, he was happy to be supported by his waitressing wife and grateful for the leftovers she brought home from work. Now that she didn't have to work, he didn't want her to. Sadly, Sasha was just as ambitious and goal-oriented as her husband, which she proved when she agreed to eat grass with him rather than sell the rights to *Rocky*. Her own career needs had to be sacrificed to her husband's personal needs. Sasha had loved shooting publicity stills on the set of *Rocky* and landed a major coup photographing her husband for his *Playboy* interview in 1978.

Sasha said she wanted to become a professional photographer, 'but Sly didn't want me to work. If I took on assignments, he knew that I would not always be available to him.' She deferred to her husband and transferred her enormous creative energy into furnishing their mansion. One morning Sasha Stallone woke up and found she was no longer her husband's partner. She had become a Hollywood wife. Although they would stay together for nearly another decade, their estrangement began when the actor squelched his wife's artistic aspirations.

While the renamed *Paradise Alley* evolved in pre-production, Stallone decided his next film would be one he didn't write. It would also contain a central character with an IQ about 100 points higher than the first film's hero.

Already a master of the one-sentence high concept film ('Shark terrorizes resort community.' 'Luxury liner sinks!'), Stallone neatly contrasted his first and second film roles. 'Rocky was a character who was led by men. In *F.I.S.T.* I play a trucker who is a leader of men.'

*F.I.S.T.* was an orphan with prestigious parents. The screenplay was by Joe Eszterhas, at the time an award-winning investigative journalist who would later pen *Flashdance* and *Basic Instinct*. The first director attached to the project, Bob Rafelson, was most famous for jump-starting Jack Nicholson's career with *Five Easy Pieces*, transforming the character actor of *Easy Rider* into a leading man. But Rafelson wanted to turn *F.I.S.T.*'s truckdriver turned union leader into an existentialist hero. United Artists fired Rafelson without even calling him personally. Sliding further down the food chain, the studio tapped Karel Reisz, best known for his collaboration with Vanessa Redgrave on *Morgan*. Reisz planned to turn the protagonist of *F.I.S.T.* into a Marxist leader. The future Rambo a commie! Mel Brooks couldn't come up with a funnier concept for a film parody.

Reisz with a paperback of *Das Kapital* under his arm returned to his native UK. The studio finally settled on a nice hybrid, Norman Jewison: a popcorn director with a taste for more than coconut oil butter and salt; an A-list filmmaker who felt comfortable sampling the guilty pleasures of B-list movie conceits. He had helped Rod Steiger win a best actor Oscar for *In the Heat of the Night* in 1967 and a year later showed a flair for stylish fluff like *The Thomas Crown Affair*. Despite Jewison's association with the project, *F.I.S.T.* remained 'in turnaround', a face-saving Hollywood euphemism for cancelled. Jewison had offered the project to Al Pacino and Jack Nicholson without results. Then he showed it to Stallone with a much better outcome. Jewison said, ' He called me the next day and told me it was one of the best scripts he had ever read and he wanted to do it.'

But even 'one of the best' could be made better, and Stallone immediately began meddling with the storyline. *Rocky* had taught him an indelible lesson. The public wants winners, not losers, on screen. His own early writing attempts had been so dark they were unproduceable. *F.I.S.T.* was also very dark. It was a thinly veiled account of Jimmy Hoffa's career in the Teamsters. The title is an acronym for the union the hero, Johnny Kovak, heads: The Federated Interstate Truckers Union. But in the draft Jewison had unsuccessfully hustled in Hollywood, Johnny was a jerk. Before signing on to the project, Stallone wanted to turn Johnny into Rocky with a union card.

'Johnny Kovak was a dastardly guy, the most rotten human being to walk the earth. At the end, when he gets killed, we would all cheer. I said I would do the picture if I could tailor the part for me,' Stallone said.

This script meddling reflects the beginning of Stallone's troubled relationships with directors. Jewison was A-list, a master of both arty action films (the chessboard seduction in *The Thomas Crown Affair*) and character-driven films that managed to fill art houses and multiplexes. With the exception of John Huston, Jewison was the classiest director Stallone would ever work with. As his box-office clout grew, Stallone's self-confidence in filmmaking grew commensurately. And so did his meddling. Eventually, Stallone ended up working with B-list, journeymen directors who were willing to defer to the superstar. This was great for the star's ego, but many industry analysts believe it also accounted for a filmography that has failed to live up to the early promise of *Rocky*.

Stallone, however, insisted that the Johnny Kovak makeover had nothing to do with ego or clout. It was for the good of the project and what the fans wanted from a Sylvester Stallone picture. An A-list director like Jewison might have the *cojones* to remind him that it would be called a 'Norman Jewison film', not a 'Sylvester Stallone film' in the credits. Instead, after *F.I.S.T.*, the star went with lesser directors who would never have the temerity to remind him of the artistic pecking order on the set. Stallone remained cock of the roost for the next two decades until *Cop Land* not only had him surrendering artistic autonomy but his washboard abs as well.

Jewison had enough clout to set his own terms. Stallone could fiddle with the script, but the director insisted on collaborating with him during the re-write. Stallone hated the collaboration, comparing it to writing under the deadline of the TV gameshow *Beat the Clock*!

Regardless of his talent as a re-write man, Stallone had learned cost-cutting from his shoestring début. Even with the star's name attached, United Artists balked at the cost of mounting a period picture spanning decades. Stallone not only cut out Kovak's emotional warts, he took a hatchet to the script, deleting enough pages to shrink the budget down to $8 million. It was an amazing feat of economy, regardless of the quality of the final draft. The original script by Joe Eszterhas would have cost $12.5 million to produce, and UA flatly rejected the budget. With a superstar and a cheaper script in tow, *F.I.S.T.* became an instant 'go'.

Stallone didn't want money for his considerable writing talent, but his hungry actor days made him a chowhound for his second starring role. His fee as an actor jumped considerably from *Rocky*'s piddling SAG minimum, with a princely half million up front, plus the now standard profit participation.

Stallone threw himself into the project, with typical intellectual and physical preparation. Besides Hoffa, he researched the lives of other labour leaders like Walter Reuther, John L. Lewis and Samuel Gompers. Despite the derision his all-protein diet for *Rocky* got from the press, Stallone also moulded his body for the new role with another unorthodox eating regimen consisting solely of bananas and water. The actor hated it, but was willing as usual to suffer for his art. 'It wasn't a laugh riot. In fact, it left me bordering on lunacy. But bananas contain potassium, which stimulates the nerve synapses.' The mineral overload, the amateur dietician insisted, made him hyperactive, just the way he wanted to play the energised union boss. Stallone was not only willing to mutate his mind for his art, he happily trashed the temple that his body had become. The banana and water diet was overhyped for its asceticism. To play the paunchy, middle-aged trucker, he binged on fattening food to develop, well, a paunch. Jealous colleagues, unaware of his weight gain's purpose, enjoyed his physical deterioration. 'Look at Stallone,' he imagined them thinking, 'he's turning into a regular warthog!'

Other people accused the star of being a 'credit hog', demanding credit as co-writer of *F.I.S.T.* When Joe Eszterhas's screenplay – the size of a telephone book, the star claimed – landed on his desk, it was a 380-page mess. It lacked structure, pacing and excitement. Stallone claimed he rewrote at least 60 per cent of Eszterhas's version without demanding a writer's cut of the profits or a piece of the novelisation of the film, which sold for a whopping $400,000.

The star brought an instant track record to his critique of Eszterhas's script. Stallone had received an Oscar nomination for *Rocky*'s screenplay. Eszterhas was a reporter for *Rolling Stone* and wrote non-fiction, specialising in a cross between investigative journalism and celebrity profiles. *F.I.S.T.* was Eszterhas's first screenplay to sell.

'This makes me so mad,' Stallone said about criticism that he had invaded Eszterhas's turf. 'I didn't want anything. Just partial credit. This project was passed on by every studio in this country and abroad. Then I rewrote it and it got made.' Stallone is, of course, being disingenuous here. Although his re-write did pare down an unfilmable script, *F.I.S.T.* got made not because of his writing genius but because of his marquee value as an actor. Movie theatres wouldn't swell with people who turned out to see a 'film written by Sylvester Stallone, Oscar-nominated for *Rocky*'. They would stand in line outside theatres, however, to see the star of *Rocky* in his next film.

For three drafts, Eszterhas received $90,000 and 2.5 per cent of the film's profits. Stallone, however, didn't want money or points for his literary contribution. *Rocky*'s continuing haul had set him up for life. At this point in his career, he wanted what no movie star mansion or Mercedes SE could bestow: respect. In particular, respect for his intelligence. He had written the character of Rocky Balboa *too* well. Fans – and more importantly, some studio executives and filmmakers whose opinion was far more important – thought Stallone *was* his monosyllabic creation with much of his grey matter destroyed in the ring, despite the fact that Stallone had never gone beyond sparring to prepare for the role. He wasn't punchy, but he feared people thought he was. And always crowding the edge of his consciousness were his father's words, transferred to *Rocky* verbatim, that his strength lay in brawn, not brains.

Stallone's fiddling with screenwriting and editing, of course, represented the power of stardom, but on a much more elemental level, his behaviour silently screamed, 'I am not the idiot dad and my teachers said I was!' To this end, the powerful star almost resorted to begging, saying, 'All I wanted was *partial* [writing] credit.'

Eszterhas refused to budge and even exacerbated the conflict by using his skills as a journalist. He went to the press with his story. Despite being a newcomer to screenwriting, Eszterhas was not about to be intimidated by a moronic Rocky Balboa or a street-smart Sylvester Stallone. He fanned the quiet brushfire by giving an interview to a local Iowa paper in which he accused the actor of trying 'to steal my script and muscle in on two years of my research, feeding his ego by getting the credit'. Eszterhas also called the star an egomaniac in the interview.

'Stallone changed a few scenes, but the concept is still mine,' he insisted. Stallone's people offered the screenwriter a deal. Stallone and Eszterhas would share screenwriting credit, Eszterhas would get sole story credit, and most important, the writer wouldn't have to share a penny of the $400,000 advance or royalties sure to pour in from his novelisation of the script. Then Stallone's lawyer threw in the deal-breaker. The actor wanted a printed apology, retracting Eszterhas's comments in the interview he gave to the Dubuque, Iowa, paper. Eszterhas summarily rejected all three elements of the deal.

The script went to the Writers Guild for arbitration, and an impartial panel of fellow writers agreed with Stallone. The final credits say screenplay by Joe Eszterhas and Sylvester Stallone. Whether or not Stallone is stupid, we'll leave to sessions with his psychotherapist. He was, however, persistent and very street-smart when it came to getting what he wanted. And an unbiased jury of his peers, perhaps even his superiors in writing, agreed that he co-wrote *F.I.S.T.*

But even validation by the respected Writers Guild didn't stop people in power from loathing Stallone and questioning his contribution to the script, despite the Guild's verdict. You can be 'right' in Hollywood, but if people don't like you, you're still 'wrong'. Wrong translates into a reputation for being difficult. And after a few flops, difficult turns into unemployable. Everyone wants to work with a temperamental superstar when his films gross $200 million per pic. But after a few *Waterworlds* or *Cutthroat Islands*, egomania isn't excusable anymore, it's pathological. And something you want to stay away from. It's no coincidence that the only acting jobs Barbra Streisand takes on these days are the ones in which she also directs. No one else will sign on for the heavy labour of directing her.

An executive, unnamed as usual, at United Artists, which had been enriched by *Rocky*, said of the fisticuffs over *F.I.S.T.*, 'Sly is a terrible pain in the ass. This whole *F.I.S.T.* nonsense is because Sly now believes that he created the whole thing, like he did with *Rocky*. It is simply not true. Sly's major contribution was that he figured out how to cut it. He brought the budget down to eight million dollars and because of this, the picture got made. He did some very intelligent editing, but it is Joe's script.'

Stallone had wrestled the script and his body exactly into the shape he wanted, but ultimately, the project turned into a personal nightmare. Or as he diplomatically put it, 'The whole experience of making *F.I.S.T.* was very unpleasant. It wasn't worth the seven months I spent making it.'

An armchair astrologer, Stallone believed in omens, and *F.I.S.T.* began with an 'ominous' one. Shortly before going on location in Iowa, he decided to pay a surprise visit to the home of his longtime manager, Jane Oliver. In a dog-eat-babies industry, Oliver stood out for her kindness and honesty. She believed in her client long before *Rocky* validated her judgement. Stallone showed his loyalty by keeping Oliver on even after his career reached a point where another superstar would have dumped her for more prestigious management, typical in the business.

Before leaving for Dubuque, Stallone showed up unannounced at Oliver's house and heard terrible news from her husband. Jane was dead. She had been suffering from cancer during the filming of *Rocky*, and she didn't want to distract her single-minded client from the fight of his life and career. Her death was the first inkling Stallone had that his beloved manager had even been ill.

Instead of being impressed with Oliver's selflessness, Stallone solipsistically complained of abandonment. In other words, how dare you leave me now, when I need you the most?

Stallone considered his manager a human gyroscope in a topsy-turvy career. He attributed many of the problems on the set of *F.I.S.T.* to the absence of his manager-armchair-therapist-anger-management-consultant and ego-wrangler. 'She was the stabilising force in my life. She was the subtle stroke. I've never been a very subtle person. So I went on a rampage when I thought I was infallible.'

Anger, not a sense of loss, accompanied him to the set in Dubuque. He'd find a lot more to vent his anger on in the Heartland.

Tired of being typecast as a monosyllabic action hero, Stallone tried to branch out with films such as *Oscar* (1991) (*above*), a comedy in which he played a lovable gangster trying to go legit, and *Tango & Cash* (1989) (*left*) in which he played an articulate cop who wears Armani suits and designer glasses
(Photofest and Everett Collection)

Stallone underwent plastic surgery to repair the damage wreaked by five *Rocky* movies.
Before . . .

. . . and after (Photofest)

Fans rejected Stallone's forays into science
fiction with (*right*) *Demolition Man*
(1993) and (*above*) *Judge Dredd* (1995)
(Photofest and Everett Collection)

*Cliffhanger* (1993) rekindled Stallone's career (Everett Collection)

Estelle Getty had the title role in *Stop! Or My Mom Will Shoot* (1992), which Stallone described as 'the most unhappy experience I ever had on a film' (Everett Collection)

Stallone reportedly felt threatened by the youth and the popularity of Antonio Banderas, his co-star in *Assassins* (1995) (Photofest)

Sharon Stone loved working with Stallone in *The Specialist* (1996) (Everett Collection)

Stallone with (*left*) Robert De Niro and (*right*) Harvey Keitel in *Cop Land* (1997). Stallone gained nearly three stone to play the overweight policeman (Everett Collection)

*Daylight* (1996) was a disaster film about a flooded tunnel in New York (Photofest)

# Chapter Six

# F.I.S.T.-icuffs

In Hollywood, insiders snickered and called Stallone the 'male Barbra Streisand', another overnight superstar who became a notorious micromanager on the set. In the boondocks, the locals didn't resort to snide analogies. The residents of Dubuque, Iowa, came to hate him, according to Jeff Rovin's 1985 insightful biography, *Stallone! A Hero's Story*.

*F.I.S.T.* provided employment for more than 500 townspeople, but money wasn't everything. Fans wanted a piece of their idol. By now, however, Stallone was tired and even fearful of smash and grab fans, especially after one of them mistook his jaw for a punching bag.

It wasn't a paranoid superstar but an assault victim who had been smacked in the face who said on the set in Dubuque, 'The security situation during the entire shooting of the film was mediocre. I was bothered all the time by fans. I know many extras thought I was stuck up, but I'm not. Hell, I was an extra myself not so long ago. But I firmly believe an actor should remain solitary if he hopes to act with 100 per cent efficiency. If I were to go around chatting, much of my energy would be skimmed off. We all have a bank of creativity, but if we use it up in idle talk, then it's wasted and we have nothing to call upon when it's really needed.'

Like a prizefighter who foregoes sex before the big match to sublimate his energy into the fight, Stallone felt chit-chat with fans would take him away from the tight-lipped, unfriendly union leader he was trying to create for *F.I.S.T.*. And this wasn't a superstar's newfound sense of self-importance and self-imposed isolation. He wasn't playing Achilles brooding in his Winnebago, refusing to come out and fight autograph-seeking Trojans. To prepare for any feat of endurance, Stallone felt obliged to distance himself from distractions. 'I've always believed that. When I used to play football, I'd never talk to a soul before a game. I knew it would sap my strength and energy.'

According to one member of the Iowa crew, however, Stallone wasn't saving himself for his art. He was hitting on a local woman this crew member had already put dibs on. 'Talk about ego,' the production worker said. The crewman invited a pretty woman he had spotted around town to visit him on the set. Stallone also liked what he saw and 'started coming on real strong', according to the crew member. The star ordered the woman to 'be in my room at eight tonight'. The woman already had a date – with the crew member. In fact, she ignored Stallone's invitation and went out with the crew member, but the actor's father tracked them down at a restaurant. Dad didn't make a scene. He simply picked up the phone and reported the tryst to his son. The next day, Stallone had his 'rival' fired. His rival's parting shot: 'He looked so foolish. He really is beginning to believe what they write about him.'

Another crew member also shielded by anonymity said, 'He's become such a bastard that even his dog Butkus turned on him and bit him.' Stallone, however, didn't have Butkus fired.

Despite their own battles, Jewison defended the star, especially his inaccessibility to fans and crew, explaining that Stallone was not doing Garbo, he was doing Jake La Motta in *Raging Bull* – keeping himself energised for the camera. Holding back until the director shouted, 'Action!', Jewison explained, allowed him to act with 'total abandonment and honesty'.

Stallone didn't return the compliment. As an unknown he still had the temerity to squabble with a veteran like John Avildsen. With *Rocky*'s box-office clout behind him, Stallone wasn't about to kowtow even to an Oscar-winning director like Jewison. But now, instead of haggling over the correct emotion of a climactic scene as in *Rocky*, Stallone allowed himself to fall into the sinkhole of superstar perks and other self-indulgences.

'I didn't think I was being treated right. Norman was staying in a $2,500-a-month house, and I was in a $70-a-week hotel, a real rat-trap. Norman's next to a country club listening to the birds, and I'm in my room listening to the pipes rattle,' Stallone said. '*F.I.S.T.* was not what you'd call a blissful experience. If I were on the set for another day or two there would have been some tremendous volcanic explosions. I couldn't have taken another day. There was no script communication after the filming started. There was no one to talk to. Nobody asked me what I thought about anything. There was never one day of rehearsal. We just walked on to the set and would wing it. I was putting on weight,' he complained, despite engineering a diet for exactly that purpose. 'I began to take the character and all of his problems home with me.'

His complaints ring hollow and suggest whining for whining's sake. At this point in his career, if Stallone had really been unhappy with his accommodation, all he had to do was pick up the phone, and his agent would have browbeaten the studio for a penthouse pad or whatever top-of-the-line housing Dubuque had to offer. And Jewison obviously didn't have problems communicating with his star, since they shared a crowded editing room together after the project wrapped.

Stallone's complaints, instead, suggest a deeply unhappy man whose disenchantment was unfocused and scattershot at any imaginary target that caught his attention. Today, it might be a verminous Motel Roach. Tomorrow, it could be haggling over a co-writer's screen credit.

The star had more profound problems with the production than his living arrangements in Dubuque. As in the case of *Rocky*, the biggest blows fell over the ending. Three different climaxes were filmed. Preview audiences would be allowed to pick the most effective.

Jewison wanted Stallone's union leader to simply disappear, in keeping with the film's *roman à clef* flavour, since Jimmy

Hoffa had met the same fate. Another ending had Stallone assassinated after testifying before Congress on organised crime's involvement with his union. Stallone, of course, favoured a virtual knockoff of *Rocky*'s triumphant ending, with Kovak standing on the Capitol steps and triumphantly raising his fist in the air. After all, the movie was called *F.I.S.T.*. All that was missing would have been Talia Shire shrieking in front of Congress, 'I love you, Rocky, uh, Johnny!' Except, of course, Shire didn't co-star.

At this point in his career, which was still on the upswing, Stallone wasn't obsessed with career-reviving sequels as he would later become. He didn't object to killing Johnny Kovak because he planned to make *F.I.S.T. II*. He simply believed the audience likes its hero alive and standing at the film's end, as *Rocky* proved. Earlier in the decade, it was practically obligatory that Faye Dunaway's character was shot in the head by her incestuous father's henchmen at the end of *Chinatown*. The country was in the middle of a recession, and the ending reflected the gloom and doom mood. When *F.I.S.T.* neared release, the economy was still a mess, but *Rocky* had given the nation hope. And now Norman Jewison, who had directed a feel-bad classic about a racist cop, *In the Heat of the Night*, was pushing for *F.I.S.T.*'s anti-hero to fade away like a trade union version of General MacArthur's old soldier. (The other ending with Kovak's assassination was killed off before it even made it to the editing room!)

But the director wasn't imperious. He showed test audiences both endings, Stallone's and his. The research was inconclusive. 'There was no difference in audience reaction to Johnny doing a disappearing act or fisting Capitol Hill,' the director said. Jewison enjoyed the ambiguity of leaving Kovak's fate unsettled at fade out.

Stallone hated ambiguity. He saw black and white, not subtle shades of grey. His ending for *F.I.S.T.*, he insisted, was 'a definite upper, just as the *Rocky* finish was. To have Kovak die is a total downer. For him to die is for the American labour movement to die; my ending has a lot to do with the American way of life, which is always to bounce back after defeat.'

Stallone was livid, even petulant, when United Artists went with Jewison's ending. 'I *wish* I had some say,' Stallone complained, 'but I don't. I must have told [Jewison] my views over 50 times, but it didn't do any good.'

While no rumours emerged that Stallone had man-handled Jewison in the editing room as he had allegedly roughed up Avildsen, the director couldn't resist making a crack about their artistic battles when Jewison appeared in public wearing a cast on his arm. 'It's not true that Sylvester Stallone broke my arm over the ending. United Artists did,' he said tongue-in-cheek, arm in shoulder sling.

The actor's professional problems began to create problems at home. He admitted that he brought job stress on the set home with him. If only he had stayed at home. After *F.I.S.T.* wrapped, Sasha returned to California, and her husband flew to New York to scout locations for his next film, *Paradise Alley*. While his extra-marital dabbling in Dubuque was discreet because of the far-off location, New York City was in the heart of tabloid land, and soon the paparazzi were shooting Stallone out on the town with other women. One regular figure in the tabs was Joyce Ingalls, his leading lady in *Paradise Alley*. Sasha had tolerated his workaholism, his curtailment of her own career to play housewife and his refusal to discuss work when he did come home, but flagrant infidelity was too much for even the co-dependent Mrs Stallone found herself becoming. In March 1978, she filed for divorce.

Long before the tabs provided photographic proof, enemies of the star on the New York set of *Paradise Alley* got their revenge by letting Sasha know about her husband's fling. She recalled her rollercoaster reaction to the news. 'At first I was frightened and distraught. Then I was furious. We had been on the bottom together and when he made it to the top he wanted to go it alone.'

Stallone feigned empathy and didn't dispute his wife's complaints about his roving eye and absence from hearth. 'I'm not the kind of guy who can fake it and pretend life at home is fine and then go out and play the field with a mistress in every port . . . My marriage was good but it was beginning to ebb.' He accepted blame. The speed of his success had gone to his head and infected his vision. 'I flipped out,' he said simply. 'I was moving on a fast track, and when you're going that fast, it's hard to keep the scenery in view – it becomes a blur.'

In divorce papers, Sasha used the typical face-saving reason for the split, 'irreconcileable differences'. Stallone was more explicit and announced 'there was something missing' in his life. With the tabloids seemingly egging both sides on, Sasha stopped being nice and began to make waves. She froze their joint bank accounts and accused her estranged husband of squandering their community property on his new leading lady.

*F.I.S.T.* came out a month after Sasha filed for divorce. Now the ravenous press had two targets to nosh on: Stallone's messy private life made public and the public failure of his first film after *Rocky*. Invidious comparisons between the two movies were inevitable. *Rocky* had grossed nearly $120 million in the US alone. *F.I.S.T.* grabbed only $20 million domestically. United Artists' cut, $9.5 million, meant the film made a tiny profit because of its $8.5 million budget, but executives at United Artists must have been wondering if all the fighting in Iowa and the editing room had been worth it.

The reviews sounded as though they had been written by disgruntled crew members on the set in Dubuque. Some critics reviewed Stallone rather than the film, an easy mistake to make since the artistic battles suggested he, not Jewison or Eszterhas, was the *auteur*.

Film critic Rex Reed wrote in the New York *Daily News*, 'Instead of a head, Sylvester Stallone carries on his shoulder an ego the size of a 40-pound eggplant.' Reed slammed Stallone for meddling with the work of a 'respected writer', Eszterhas, even though Eszterhas had earned his respect as a journalist, not as a tiro screenwriter. 'Stallone has turned a viable story of union corruption into a massive ego massage without the talent to back it up.' Reed was also the first, but not the last, to complain about the actor's 'droning monotone' voice.

*Newsweek* alliterated that *F.I.S.T.* was 'big, bold and botched'. And like Rex Reed, the magazine put the blame on the star, not the director or that *other* writer. 'A great actor might have made

Johnny Kovak into an authentic tragic hero. Sylvester Stallone is not that actor.'

The *New York Times*'s Vincent Canby, who hadn't been impressed with Rocky Balboa or his *avatar*, actually liked Johnny Kovak and the actor who had re-written him. The union leader, Canby, enthused, 'is played by Sylvester Stallone with a combination of brute power and arrogance that are convincing'.

*Variety* agreed, although its praise for Stallone's performance ('great as the corrupt union leader') was undercut by the trade paper's prediction that the film's box-office performance would not match its star's acting performance.

Perhaps the negative reviews had a sobering effect. Or maybe he was just lonely. But Stallone took the occasion of the film's New York première to make amends in a big way. Although he had been so unhappy with the final cut he had refused to do any interviews to promote *F.I.S.T.*, he did turn up at the première – with his estranged wife on his arm! To get the biggest bang for his publicity buck, Stallone announced in front of flashing paparazzi and scribbling reporters that Sasha had dropped the divorce proceedings. He took full responsibility for 'having destroyed the tranquility of my family and publicly embarrassing my wife and friends'.

Sasha told the crowd at the première, 'We got together the evening before.' Stallone was so happy (maybe he hadn't seen the reviews), he also used the première to make another apology – to Eszterhas – this after challenging him to a fistfight when the Iowa newspaper interview came out. 'We had a clash of egos. I feel as though I was robbing his house,' the actor said about his co-writer.

The reconciliation was just the climactic public act to a private wooing that had gone on for months. After she filed for divorce, Sasha flew to Philadelphia for her sister's wedding. Stallone was too busy working on his new film in New York to join Sasha for the wedding, but he pursued her with flowers and phone calls on a daily basis. And he stopped dancing in nightclubs with his leading lady. Stallone begged for a second chance, and Sasha caved.

Soon, Stallone was flying back to LA to spend three or four days a week with his wife and the baby, probably more time together than before she filed for divorce. It was a strange estrangement. Public infidelity and humiliation hadn't affected their physical affection for one another. Sasha said, 'Our sex life was still passionate, and he was still very attached to the baby.' Stallone also stopped criticising his wife, which in retrospect she believed was simply her husband projecting his own self-loathing and career drift on to her.

Sasha took him back, but on new, self-liberating terms. Stallone got to keep his wife. She got to keep her career as a budding photographer with assignments backed up into the next decade. 'There was a part of me that wanted freedom too,' she said. And her husband, realising how much he had come to love a woman he had taken for granted, forced himself to abandon his Neanderthal concept of stay-at-home moms and wives. In fact, his dependence on Sasha's emotional support was so great, the separation lasted only four months.

And it was Stallone who ate crow, picked up the phone and begged to be taken back. Sasha said he 'called and said he wanted to come over to discuss our future. He came over and said he needed his roots; the baby and I were his foundation. He wanted to come home to stay.' Stallone implied his wife understated his longing for a reconciliation with a woman he had so much history with. Their four-month split seemed like an eternity, and only pride had kept them apart that long. 'I wanted to go home badly. But I waited and waited for the proper opportunity – until I realised there is no such thing. You just have to strip yourself down to the bare wires and do it.'

Their reconciliation was aided by the fact that during the estrangement she acceded to her husband's demand that she did not date other men while he dallied with Joyce Ingalls. Double standards die hard. Sasha didn't object, saying, 'Sly would be a hard act to follow.' In a neat book-ending of infidelity and fidelity, soon the tabloids were filled with photos of Stallone and his wife dancing at Xenon, the hot New York nightclub. Joyce Ingalls was out of the picture. She may have wished she was out of that other picture, *Paradise Alley*.

Stallone's eye had originally begun to wander as he looked at his leading lady on the set of *Paradise Alley*. Perhaps he needed the distraction from the business of movie-making, especially since he not only starred but also directed and wrote the film, based on his critically mauled novel.

Filming *Paradise Alley* began under an omen almost as awful as Jane Oliver's death just before *F.I.S.T.* went into production. The critics already hated the source of the screenplay, Stallone's novelisation of the script he had written years before under the title of *Hell's Kitchen*. Hey, if *F.I.S.T.*'s novelisation could earn Eszterhas almost half a million dollars, why shouldn't Stallone cash in on his first stab at the printed page?

The *New York Times* summed up the critical consensus on Sylvester Stallone, novelist: 'Mr Stallone has no verbal imagination whatever.'

To take the fuel out of the plagiarism suit filed by the producers who had purchased the rights to *Paradise Alley* when it was called *Hell's Kitchen* and also to avoid accusations he was overfishing stale waters, Stallone re-wrote the story. He took it out of contemporary New York and relocated it in the late 1940s. He also relocated it in the world of wrestling. And this time, Stallone was not the fighter. His dim-witted younger brother, played by boxing hopeful Lee Canalito, played the rope-a-dope wrestler. Stallone played one of Canalito's two siblings. His character in *Paradise Alley*, Cosmo Carboni, was sharper than Rocky Balboa by about 100 IQ points. Cosmo hoped to use his brother's physical prowess to lift all three Carbonis out of the slums. It was *Rocky* in the wrestling ring without *Rocky*'s uplifting message. Also, unfortunately without *Rocky*'s revenues or reviews.

If *F.I.S.T.* had been a small boating disaster with the press and public, *Paradise Alley* was a Titanic failure, grossing less than half *F.I.S.T.*'s tepid box-office. The critical fury contrasted with the public indifference, but with the same results. Word of mouth and the printed word killed *Paradise Alley* when it opened in November 1978.

As writer-director-star, Stallone couldn't blame anybody but himself. If there had been fights in the editing room, he must have been beating himself up – punishment perhaps for viewing on the movieola what he had created on the set.

*Time* magazine knew where to point the finger and place the blame. *Time*'s film critic, Frank Rich, wasn't the first to diagnose a terminal case of Streisand Syndrome. 'As an exercise in egomania, *Paradise Alley* almost puts Barbra Streisand's *A Star Is Born* to shame.' The comparison, however, was inaccurate in one important area. People tolerated Streisand's demanding diva because her films made money. *A Star Is Born* grossed more than $100 million in the US alone. *Paradise Alley* hit a dead end at $6.5 million.

Even fans of his acting deserted him after only three forays in front of the camera. *The New Yorker*'s Pauline Kael had adored *Rocky*, but now it was time to retire his fists and smash Sasha's typewriter, the critic suggested. 'As a writer he's a primitive, mining the mass media without any apparent awareness of how stale his ideas are . . . It's not as if Stallone didn't have some talent . . . But after three starring roles, Stallone's limitations as an actor have become apparent.'

The nastiest review practically called for public castration of the *auteur*, only higher up on the anatomy. 'He's taken every bad habit since film began, and made it worse . . . We could only recommend that he cut his vocal chords and stand as far away as he can in a crowd scene,' Kael wrote. Is it any wonder that during a TV talk show appearance at this time, Stallone challenged a film critic to a fistfight?

Only *Newsweek*'s Jack Kroll stayed in Rocky's corner: 'I'm for Sylvester Stallone. As a performer, he has that rare treasure: comical power. As a filmmaker, he is engagingly arrogant and he gives lots of screen time to an army of appealing new performers.'

Stallone reacted to the film's failure in a way that seems irrational. He blamed it on the stars. Not his co-stars, the stars in the sky. He claimed three astrologers (but failed to mention if mom was one of them) had warned him not to release *Paradise Alley* in November because the stars were out of alignment. His argument wasn't quite so preposterous since another astrological prediction, provided by his mother, had accurately foretold the time and nature of his success: seven years and screenwriting.

Whether these excuses represented navel-gazing or star-gazing became irrelevant. Stallone had something to take his mind off the vilification in the press and the boycott at the box-office. When *Paradise Alley* came out to a hellish reception, he was already at work on a film that would put him back on top. And he would prove that writing, directing and starring were not too many hats to wear for someone with as big a head as his. One man's Streisand Syndrome is another man's Cruise on the Cameron Line, a nasty diva or the king of the hill.

# Chapter Seven

# Roman Numerology

Although no one, including the star himself, would have thought so at the time, Stallone was one lucky fellow. Before *Paradise Alley* hit a dead end, United Artists had already agreed to a sequel to *Rocky*. In fact, the studio was even luckier than the star, since it had secured his services for *Rocky II* at the same time he signed for the original and for considerably less money than the post-*Rocky* superstar might have demanded.

Stallone had a deal, but he also had a dilemma. What to do for an encore. Some of the ideas he toyed with suggest a superstar out of touch, if not with reality, at least with realism. One rejected storyline had Rocky retiring from the ring, attending night school, entering politics and cleaning up Congress. Mr Balboa Goes to Washington, a concept from hell if ever there was one.

On a slightly less grandiose scale, which would later be shrunk to fit something resembling reality, Rocky would return to the ring and wrest the title from Apollo Creed. So far, so good. But Stallone wanted to stage the climactic fight in the Roman Colosseum, a scarier thought than Stallone as a muscular version of Jimmy Stewart filibustering the Senate. Another idea would have plagiarised another one of his scripts about a humble cab driver who runs for mayor of Philadelphia, with the cabbie metamorphosing into Rocky Balboa. Ding!

Even before *Paradise Alley*'s release questioned Stallone's talent for directing, he wanted John Avildsen back in the director's chair for *Rocky II*. Unfortunately, Avildsen had an idea for the sequel so un-*Rocky*-like that the Colosseum and Congressional scenarios seemed attractive by comparison. With the instant clout bestowed by a best director Oscar, Avildsen wanted Rocky to become a drug addict in his return to the screen and the ring. The sound of theatre box-office windows slamming shut all over America could be heard as Avildsen pitched the idea to UA and Stallone.

Avildsen's cockeyed scenario gave Stallone an excuse to do what he already wanted to: cleanse himself of his writing failure with *F.I.S.T.* and his directing fiasco on *Paradise Alley*. He would take on the Triple Crown and perform all three tasks, including of course, star.

The final draft, which began shooting in October 1978, didn't stray too far from the elements that had made the original a pop culture and box-office phenomenon. Rocky marries Adrian and accedes to her demand to give up boxing because it's so dangerous. Rocky leaves the ring and returns to his blue-collar roots. His low-earning job can't pay Adrian's enormous medical bills when the birth of Rocky Jr, eerily echoing Stallone's own traumatic birth, puts Adrian into a coma. (Trivia fans note: the hospital bedside scene is the first and only time Stallone ever cries in a movie. In a rare revelation of weakness, Stallone confessed that he not only hates crying on screen, but finds it hard to summon up tears on cue.)

Although Apollo Creed won the fight in the original, Rocky went the distance and in the sequel Creed feels his title lacks credibility. Carl Weathers's brilliant performance as an even more extroverted Ali includes public taunts, calling Rocky a 'chicken' and demanding a re-match. The pressure of hospital bills and public humiliation proves too much, and surprise! Rocky returns to the ring.

How do you make a re-match original? Spend eight times the original budget. Stallone wanted to keep the sequel low budget and retain the gritty flavour of the original. Ironically, after its parsimony about filming the first *Rocky*, United Artists practically stuffed $8 million down his throat, or at least on to the screen, a massive eight-fold increase on the original.

The money didn't go for the star's salary, which had been negotiated at the same time as the first film. It was all up there on the screen . . . and in the sound effects. Most of *Rocky*'s fight scenes had been shot from low angles to hide the fact that the filmmakers couldn't afford to hire extras for this alleged 'fight of the century'. For the sequel, money was found to pack, if not the Roman Colosseum, a venue almost as large. Expensive sound effects made the thud of fists to the face sound like Sensurround and earned the critics' derision. But the audience loved physical abuse in Dolby.

The bigger budget created problems of its own. More money meant more cameras. The fight scenes had six going at once, plus an additional one for slow motion. Putting this all together was so exhausting – plus he didn't have John Avildsen to hurl against the wall for relaxation – that Stallone claimed he had to be carried out of the editing room by two men hired by the studio so the film could make its June 1979 release date.

Until Stallone broke the rule himself with *Rambo*, sequels never make more money than the original. They are considered a hit if they do 60 per cent of the first film's business. *Rocky II* earned 90 per cent of *Rocky*'s take, $79 million. This time, the reviews, which were even more sulphurous than his previous notices, barely diluted the euphoria of the box-office news. His failure to earn an Oscar nomination did sting, however, since after three starring roles, he felt his acting talent had increased exponentially. The Academy of Motion Pictures Arts and Sciences begged to differ. And it wasn't a case of prejudice against sequels since a second instalment about other wilful Italians, *The Godfather II*, had collected more Oscars than the original.

But an even more powerful balm against the barbs of critics and Oscar, even perhaps more analgesic than *Rocky II*'s commercial success, had to be news from home. A month before *Rocky II* opened, Sasha gave birth to their second son with the impossible to spell but easy to pronounce name Seargeoh (call him 'Sergio'). Nicknamed 'Seth', their second son had been conceived shortly after his parents' much publicised reconciliation. Seargeoh was truly a 'love' child.

Stallone joked that he planned to have all his children's first names begin with the letter 'S', a promise he would continue to keep two decades later when daughters, Sophia and Sistine, were born. 'We wanted all 'S's' in our family,' he joked. 'It's amazing what you do when you don't have a hobby!'

Stallone pointedly refused to name his kids after himself. First, he knew what it was like to grow up with kids making cracks about Tweety Bird's tormentor. Also, growing up under the onus of being Sylvster Stallone Jr was too much too bear for anybody he loved. And recalling his own childhood brawls, he feared kids would pick a fight with his sons to prove their dad wasn't so tough after all. He wanted his offspring 'to know they're individuals', not 'the son of . . .'

While the bliss of their reconciliation may have facilitated the conception of Seargeoh, his birth failed to hold the couple together. Two months after the delivery, Stallone had left Sasha again for another woman. And this time, he moved considerably higher up the pecking order of successful actresses.

Susan Anton was a gorgeous, 29-year-old former supermodel just launching her film career with a sports drama called *Goldengirl*. She was in New York doing publicity for the feature at the same time Stallone was hustling *Rocky II* there. They met on the dance floor of Studio 54 and exchanged a few words but nothing more. As Anton explained, both were married, she for four years to her manager, Jack Stein. 'Neither Sly nor I were looking to meet other people, to end our marriages. But it just happened.'

That wasn't Stallone's agenda, and he frankly admitted the success of *Rocky II* had gone to his head and parts further south. 'I got stroked [praised] so much I felt like an 185-pound blister . . . [I had] 360-degree vision. I saw everything around me, and the last place I wanted to be was at home stifled with the responsibility of a wife and two kids.'

Anton didn't make much of their first meeting at Studio 54, but the next day, when she found herself on the same LA-bound flight as Stallone, there seemed to be some karmic connection between the muscular superstar and the leggy actress, who towered over him by two inches. 'There was an instant communication,' she said of their second run-in. 'One of those amazing clicks.' They kept on clicking. Every time they met, Anton says they fell a little bit more in love.

Stallone soon moved out of the Pacific Palisades mansion which housed his wife, their new-born son and his sibling. Sasha refiled for divorce. Stallone and Anton found a beach house in Malibu with three and a half acres to provide some distance from prying eyes. Anton called this large love nest a 'little slice of heaven'. She also considered herself a moral person and planned to marry her Malibu beau as soon as his divorce from Sasha became final. 'Sly is very moral,' Anton believed. 'He wouldn't have it any other way. Eventually I want to have a child with him; and family is very important to both of us.'

Stallone had other ideas. Just as filming *Rocky II* far away from home had damaged his relationship with Sasha, his next assignment took him away from Anton. While he was making *Nighthawks* in New York, Anton stayed in LA and soon found herself out of the picture. The ballyhooed romance which had been double-trucked across tabloids around the world was over after only nine months. The relationship chiefly foundered, though, because unlike his wife, his girlfriend refused to give up her career.

His troubled lovelife would pale in comparison to the troubled path his career took at this time. *Nighthawks* would turn into a nightmare. The concept sounded good on paper. Stallone would dump his grunt-and-mumble acting style to play an articulate, college-educated cop, Sgt Deke Da Silva, whose beat is urban terrorism.

Billy Dee Williams, still hot from two *Star Wars*, got to play the totemic black sidekick. Dutch actor Rutger Hauer gave Stallone a run for his money in the handsome leading man category as a German terrorist named Wulfgar. Stallone didn't feel threatened by this Aryan stud. In fact, he decided to hire Hauer as soon as they met, even before the actor read any lines for the audition. *Nighthawks*' producer Martin Poll said he and the star both agreed the 'eyes have it'. Hauer's piercing baby blues were just the right shade of ice to play a terrorist. Poll said,

'The minute we met him, Sly and I looked at each other and nodded.' TV's Bionic bimbo, Lindsay Wagner, got the thankless wife-in-jeopardy role, while Persis Khambatta, her hair newly regrown after playing a bald Vulcan in *Star Trek: The Motion Picture*, had a meatier role as Hauer's co-terrorist.

Stallone as usual threw himself into his new role physically and mentally. He grew a lush beard and let his hair grow shoulder-length. Cast and crew nicknamed him 'Baby Jesus'. The star lost 35 pounds of muscle and adopted a cop's diet of high-fat McDonald's cuisine. He cruised the mean streets of Manhattan in decoy cop cars. Posing as feckless civilians, one cop would allow himself to get mugged, then his colleagues would grab the perpetrator. Stallone got close to one cop, only to learn later that the man had been killed doing decoy duty. It added resonance to his own scenes playing a decoy, but the emotional cost must have made him wonder if such in-depth research was worth the toll.

Once the cameras started rolling, the problems only increased. Producer Poll, not Stallone, as reported in the press, decided to fire director Gary Nelson and replace him with Bruce Malmuth after only one scene had been shot. The expensive cast and crew were kept waiting while Malmuth flew in from Los Angeles. In order not to waste a day's worth of shooting, Stallone stepped in as substitute director – for only 24 hours.

The Directors Guild threw a tantrum. In order to prevent temperamental stars from wresting control of a project away from the director, union rules forbid this kind of pinch-hitting. Although Stallone only directed one scene before Malmuth arrived, the DGA fined the production $50,000. The fine was actually a bargain, since shutting down production for even one day would have cost twice that. The New York *Daily News* had a different take on Stallone's cost-saving intervention, attributing his takeover to ego rather than economy.

Stallone averted a shutdown that time, but the next obstacle did make filming come to a halt. For a crucial sequence aboard an aerial tram connecting Manhattan to Roosevelt Island, the production paid a handsome fee to residents who would have to find other means of transportation during the shooting. Some residents considered the fee a bribe and demanded more. They got a court order and filming was stopped. Stallone tried to mediate with the *ad hoc* group of protestors who, along with the press, condemned the star for siding with a big studio (Universal) instead of the little guys (them). They expected him to play Rocky, not movie mogul.

A judge denied the petition and *Nighthawks* resumed filming aboard the tram. The moral and legal victory didn't improve his mental state, which began to deteriorate during the shoot. Anton was gone, and he missed Sasha. The attacks by the public and press also disillusioned him, and he began to self-medicate with food. The original Big Mac attack to look like a fleshy undercover cop turned into a full scale battle against the bulge. The body that had been so lovingly toned since adolescence was turning to fat. He put back on the 35 pounds and added 30 more, ballooning up to 205 pounds, more than he had ever weighed in his life. When in top shape, Stallone tickled the scales at a mere 185 pounds.

Principal photography had been a nightmare of logistics, personal deterioration and ugly battles in court and on the set. Hauer and Stallone tried to act each other off the screen. Fortunately, they only fought when the director yelled, 'Action,' and their competition actually enriched their scenes together, but Stallone found the daily battle against the suave Hauer a daily grind. His relationship with charmer Billy Dee Williams was happier. Williams said they 'got along great and had lots of fun'. Although Stallone could be a handful as a demanding perfectionist, Williams pronounced the star 'quite brilliant'.

The problems with *Nighthawks* only got worse in post-production. The editing room became yet another battleground between director and star. Stallone was horrified, watching the rough cut, to discover that Hauer not only got more screen time, but he got to do showier things, like blow up buildings and slaughter innocent bystanders. Stallone demanded Hauer's screen presence reduced and his own scenes emphasised. Producer Poll found an ingenious way to appear to placate his star. He assembled a second cut that pleased Stallone, then showed both cuts to preview audiences, who voted overwhelmingly for less Stallone, more Hauer. The studio heeded the voice (and post-screening opinion cards) of the people. The director's Hauer-heavy cut hit theatres.

It was probably a minor victory for the actor that *Nighthawks* bombed when it came out in April 1981. He could attribute its embarrassing US gross of only $14 million to his diminished presence on screen. But still, it was his name up there on screen. The public perception – and more importantly, the industry view – was that Stallone had starred in a major turkey.

After *Nighthawks* and *l'affaire* Anton completed 'production', Stallone was off to Hungary to make *Victory*, a World War II feel-good drama about soccer-playing prisoners of war. *Victory* seemed like a winner. John Huston, one of the greatest directors of all time – and certainly the best Stallone would ever collaborate with – signed on to direct. The star of popcorn classics found himself working with the *auteur* of timeless classics like *The Maltese Falcon* and *The African Queen*.

Besides the gilt-edged talent behind the camera, the story also intrigued him with its *Rocky*-esque theme of POWs who, overmatched against professional German soccer players, use the big game as cover for a successful escape. Stallone couldn't resist the parallels between his greatest hits (his only to date, in fact) and *Victory*'s theme. 'The last 20 minutes of the film are like the fight in *Rocky* with the underdog going for the big fella,' he said. Indeed, Rocky Balboa only had to fight a loud-mouthed boxer. Stallone's PoW took on the Third Reich . . . and won! His co-stars, like the director, also represented a step up in the food chain of Hollywood's dog-eat-dog casting coups. Ingmar Bergman's alter ego, the great Max von Sydow, played the camp commandant and Michael Caine, who always makes his co-stars look good, was the good guys' soccer coach. A real life soccer legend, Pele, added glamour and beefed up the film's international appeal and box-office potential.

Unlike his other films, *Victory* was a happy set. Stallone knew the director's pedigree and stayed out of Huston's artistic way. Even so, not meddling took a superhuman effort on the part of the star. 'Once you've directed, you want to constantly suggest things,' he said. He apparently kept his mouth shut. Huston, not exactly famous as a touchy-feely handler of temperamental stars, confirmed Stallone's hands-off attitude. 'I'd heard about Sly's reputation for throwing his weight around, but his behaviour here has been as modest as one could hope for. He couldn't be more disciplined.'

Stallone had a lot less weight to throw around, literally. As usual, he found his character's soul through his body and diet. He subsisted on what he called a PoW's ration of 200 calories a day: 'pure protein foods' with an occasional potato 'to keep my brain from turning to fudge'. You wonder where Stallone does his research on food groups. PoWs and concentration camp inmates rarely got protein-rich food because it costs more than starchy stuff like potatoes. And carbohydrates tend to slow the mental process, not protein. But despite his shaky knowledge of nutrition, Stallone did know how to diet his way to physical perfection. He lost all the fat purposely and accidentally gained for the fleshy cop in *Nighthawks* and starved himself down to 159 pounds for the gaunt look of a PoW.

Starvation was one of the easier sacrifices he made for 'art'. Getting punched by professional football player Carl Weathers was like a love tap compared to the abuse he took as the soccer team's goalie in *Victory*. Although the star tends to dramatise on-the-job hazards in most of his work, *Victory* sounded more punishing than any of his fight films. After a few weeks of filming, he called himself a 'walking blood clot. So far, I've broken one finger, the others are bent, and I've had injections and water removed from both knees. It's just incredible, a very tough sport.' All these sports injuries could have and should have been avoided. A severely injured star is more than a personal dilemma. He can shut down a production. Stallone should have used a stunt double for the dangerous goalie shots, but he got into an amiable macho contest with co-star Caine, who had played soccer as a schoolboy. The British actor didn't use a stuntman, and Stallone decided to do his own stunts.

The physical pain hurt less than the emotional scars left by his estrangement from Sasha. Alone in a dreary Stalinist country, Stallone decided he wanted Sasha back. Actually, he wanted her in Hungary.

The actor became philosophical when he described the durability of their on-again-off-a-*lot* marriage, dipping into automobile analogies to compare Anton and Sasha. His version of *auto*eroticism: 'Let me put it on a real crass level. Love is like a new car. The leather smells great for a while, and it's so exciting to drive it around and show it off to your people. You keep it shined and polished. You make love to it. Eventually, it gets *old*. But you know what? As long as it keeps running and it's reliable, you keep it around. You change the tyres, keep it tuned up, and it's reliable. OK, *that's* love.'

When he phoned Sasha from Budapest, we don't know if he wooed his wife back by using the old car/new car symbolism, but whatever he said to her, it worked. Sasha was just about to board a plane for a Hawaiian vacation. Instead, she joined her husband on the freezing set of *Victory* outside Budapest.

Stallone chose a romantic location to beg for Sasha's forgiveness, the banks of the river Danube, which bisects Buda and Pest. He didn't have to beg for her to come back since she was already there, but he did tell her, 'You're looking at a fully grown fool. You have every reason to despise me.' Sasha's forgiveness, he claimed, demonstrated that 'our marriage was right in the first place'.

While Hungary was the site of his reconciliation, the Communist country had an even more profound effect on his political ideology and film career. Before Hungary personally introduced him to the Orwellian world of Eastern Europe, Stallone considered himself politically neutral. Rocky stood for so many things, he could be embraced by people at all points on the political spectrum. After a few months with Big Brother watching – and listening – Stallone turned into a Red Baiter. Baiting Reds, in fact, would turn out to be one of his smartest career moves.

Besides being followed, which was standard for foreigners pre-Gorbachev and *glasnost*, Stallone felt sure his hotel room was bugged. Before Sasha flew in to make up, there wasn't much going on in his hotel room anyway, so the actor shrugged off the intrusion. But he claimed that the following day after a night of lovemaking with his wife, the hotel staff would smirk at the couple in the lobby. Big Brother became Stallone's new *bête noire*, and he would fight various Communist incarnations for much of the '80s, in perfect synch with the Reagan era.

'Budapest is so alien to me. It's a very lonely place, and I feel great empathy with these people. The police have keys to everyone's house; they can turn off all the electricity in a city if they don't like what's going on. And every couple of months the tanks run down the streets, just to remind people that they're there. To this day, I believe all our hotel rooms were bugged. If you had an amorous night with your wife, you'd walk downstairs the next morning and everyone would be grinning,' he said.

As much as he loathed Communism, it also intrigued him. To that end, he asked for a visa to the Soviet Union, which was denied. This was pre-*Rambo* and pre-*Rocky IV*, in which Balboa beat the stuffing out of a steroided Russian boxer, so the Soviet rejection was puzzling. But not to Stallone, who felt Rocky Balboa's empowering belief in himself threatened the Leninist-Stalinist concept of subverting the individual for the good of the collective. Back in the good old US of A, Stallone sounded like a Malibu version of Joe McCarthy: a two-week stay in a Communist country, he declared, would turn everyone into a Cold Warrior. 'Patriotism in America would reach epidemic proportions,' he said.

Unfortunately, his enthusiasm for *Victory* didn't prove contagious with the public. The film débuted in October 1981 with even more poisonous reviews than *Nighthawks*. And this was not a 'critic-proof' movie, with *Victory* going down to defeat even more abysmally than *Nighthawks* did. (Only $10 million for the the soccer film compared to $14 million for the cop flick.) The public had rejected him as a smart, college-educated detective. Fans hated him even more in any sporting venue other than the ring.

Stallone saw the writing on the wall – actually in *Variety*'s weekly film grosses. He had planned to take off time from acting to polish his dream project, the Edgar Allan Poe bio-pic. Instead, the scared star found himself performing emergency surgery on a career that appeared down for the count. Two flops in a row terrified a career-obsessed individual who had shown no trepidation about being smacked in the face or kicked by a professional soccer player. Or, as he succinctly explained the reason for his next film project, 'I don't want to blow what I've got.'

## Chapter Eight

# The Ring Cycle Continues

The troubled actor only had to look at his filmography to figure out what was wrong with his career. His only blockbusters had been the two *Rocky* films. Audiences didn't want to see the world's most famous fictional heavyweight champ beating up Germans, whether they were Nazis or Rutger Hauer's modern-day terrorist.

A risk-taker who thrived on challenges, the writer-director-superstar would have preferred to play a consumptive Edgar Allan Poe. He had already starved himself down to 159 pounds on a Weight Watchers From Hell diet. Another 20 pounds would have been a piece of cake, or more likely, a plate of vegetables.

United Artists encouraged his artistic conservatism. The studio ignored the back-to-back failures and wrote a cheque for $15 million in return for Stallone's services as writer, director and title star in the third instalment of Philadelphia's favourite fictional citizen. Plus, a generous slice of the profits.

The star didn't agree to the trequel for financial reasons, however. With his previous profit participation, Stallone could have spent the rest of his life happily starving his body into perfect shape at his home gym in Malibu. But just because you're rich doesn't mean you suddenly lose a lifetime habit of hard work and goal-completion. To be happy, he had to work. Plus, the third *Rocky* offered him a shot at the Triple Crown a third time: 'I didn't know if I'd ever get the chance to write, direct, and act in the same film again,' he said.

In some ways, the plot of *Rocky III* was autobiographical. In others, it was pure fiction. By now, Rocky Balboa has become soft, unlike his 159-pound interpreter, who lost an additional five pounds and dropped his body fat to a cadaverous four per cent. Unlike the career-nervous Stallone, Rocky has become complacent by now. His manager Mickey, unknown to the champ, has been matching him up against fighters who are literally knockovers. When Rocky learns the real reason he's stayed on top of his game, he decides to risk everything – unlike Stallone.

He finds an opponent worthy of himself in a psycho contender, Clubber Lang, played by an unknown who would become an overnight star, Mr T. In a stab at *cinéma vérité*, Stallone had originally planned to cast a real-life professional. But after 'auditioning' Ernie Shavers and Joe Frazier in the ring and suffering painful injuries, he decided to forego realism for the sake of self-preservation. It was a wise move for other than health reasons. Professional athletes make lousy actors.

Instead, Stallone hired a professional bouncer and bodyguard, Lawrence Tyro, the two-time winner and current title-holder of America's Toughest Bouncer. Fighting, bouncing actually, under the professional name of Mr T, the six-foot-one monster won the contest by hurling a stuntperson 14 feet. *Rocky III*'s casting director, Ronda Young, saw the match on TV and sent Mr T seven pages of the script, which consisted largely of Clubber Lang making threats like, 'I'll bust you up,' and 'I'll break your arm in six places.' He rehearsed the lines for hours every day before the audition in New York, where he found himself in a much tougher competition than Toughest Man in America. Fifteen hundred other hopefuls turned out for the role of Clubber.

The other 1,499 hopefuls could have stayed home. Stallone attended the audition and liked Mr T's exotic look, which one critic described as belonging to a man who buys his jewellery at a hardware store. Stallone took T aside and whispered, 'If you make a mistake, we'll do it again.' Only four pages into seven's worth of 'I'm going to bust you up,' Stallone had had enough . . . and Mr T had the career-making role.

During the audition, the star had been supportive and encouraging. After that, he turned into a Weight Watchers dietitian on steroids. The first thing Stallone did was put the beefy Mr T on a severe diet, which melted off 20 pounds. Now a relatively svelte 210, Mr T still outweighed Stallone by 60 pounds and towered over him, five feet ten to six feet one. His opponent's physical superiority was calculated. When Rocky eventually triumphs over Clubber Lang, the feat is all the more impressive because he's whipped a bigger guy. (In real life, a parallel universe to Hollywood make-believe, a 150-pound fighter would never be allowed in the same ring with a 210-pound monster. Or, as one visitor to the set said of the unlikely pairing, 'I've heard of fighting out of your class, but never fighting out of your species!')

With Clubber providing distilled evil, Apollo Creed's former incarnation became superfluous. So Carl Weathers's loud-mouthed ex-champ turns into a good guy in *Rocky III* and coaches his former nemesis to battle Lang, who is even scarier than the beef carcass-punching Rocky of the first film.

For all his macho posturing and muscle-flexing in public, Stallone has never been afraid to admit to raw, primal fear. That's exactly what he felt fighting Mr T. The punches were choreographed to be pulled, but as Stallone said, 'Miss a step, and you're in for a detached retina.' Mr T became a Method actor, and his Method was madness. It scared Stallone. During the climactic bout, Mr T went berserk, and his opponent confessed, 'There were moments when I was overwhelmed with real fear. When the pounding was over, I ached for weeks.'

(Trivia fans checking out the credits will note two interesting facts. Butkus, Stallone's real-life bull mastiff who played Rocky's companion in the first film, is missing. He wasn't fired by a temperamental director. Butkus had died shortly before filming began. Stallone was so depressed he couldn't bring himself to cast another dog and wrote Butkus out of the script. He did write a small part for his son Sage, who was typecast as Rocky's offspring. Burgess Meredith, who plays Rocky's trainer Mickey, dies of a heart attack after becoming overexcited by the champ's triumph over Clubber. This would become a bittersweet tradition in following instalments: a much beloved supporting character would get offed in the course of the film to provide a dramatic, some felt bathetic, death scene – Weathers would get the hook in the next *Rocky*. Talia Shire must have cringed every time the latest *Rocky* script was sent to her, flipping through it to see if this one contained *her* big death scene. So far, the writer has spared his leading lady's life.)

For a brief, crazed moment, Stallone even toyed with killing Rocky in this film. He imagined a scene, after the fight, where Rocky, overcome with the same excitement that stops Mickey's heart, puts his head on Adrian's shoulder and says, 'I'm so tired. Can I use your shoulder for a second?' The second would literally turn into an eternity, as the champ departed for that big boxing ring in the sky.

That, of course, was a daydream, and a nightmare for MGM, which had bought United Artists and was experiencing major financial problems after big budget, big star failures like *Pennies from Heaven* and *The Formula*. MGM wasn't about to kill off a franchise it hoped to milk through the millennium, and Stallone considered his creation a safety net that he could always fall back on when his other films flopped.

The star's deathbed fantasy almost became reality while shooting a training sequence which had him swimming laps. In mid-take, the star collapsed in the water and crawled out of the pool. Lying on a towel on the deck, he went into shock. His skin turned stark white and his temperature dropped while his heartbeat raced.

'My heart was doing 210 beats a minute,' he said. (A healthy pulse rate is 78.) 'The paramedics gave me oxygen, covered me in ice, then wrapped me in towels. That was the only time in my life that I was *really* frightened. My body seemed to be saying, "I can't take it anymore, Stallone, you've pushed me to the limit. I quit."'

Typically, Stallone was deaf to his body language. Fortunately, the pool scene was the last sequence shot in the film. Stallone 'recuperated' in the editing room, not wanting to miss the release date over a simple matter like a near fatal heart attack.

*Rocky III* enjoyed triple the budget of the first instalment, but took only two months to film, compared to the original's lightning strike of 30 days. Stallone said he liked to shoot fast. Maybe he really wanted to limit the time he spent getting beat up by the real Toughest Man in America.

It turned out fans loved to see their hero slaughtered – as long as he won in the end. They may also have liked the 'new, improved' star. Anyone who followed the films saw that in the third instalment Stallone had traded in his fleshier incarnation for a ripped physique that seemed to live at the gym. Novelist and boxing fancier Joyce Carol Oates sniffed that this Rocky didn't have a boxer's body; he looked like a competitive bodybuilder. Fans, of course, by now didn't want verisimilitude in this mythic ring cycle. Stallone's idealised muscles, which seemed to become more Michelangelo-esque with each screen appearance, perfectly matched the idealised hero.

More observant fans, however, noticed a subtler change in Stallone, which probably affected the actor more psychologically than his new set of muscles. To repair injuries from earlier films, Stallone underwent eye surgery. While he was under the knife, the doctors also repaired his drooping eyelid, which had been caused by the clumsy intern during his delivery and which had caused so much ridicule from peers during his formative years. Before and after photos show why cosmetic surgery is a billion-dollar business in the US. Pre-*Rocky III*, Stallone had, at best, rough-hewn good looks. In the posters for *Rocky III*, a matinee idol with a body by Fischer and cheekbones by Caravaggio peers out at us.

*Rocky III* premièred in May 1982, and the fighter from Philly saved the studio that had given us Scarlett O'Hara, Dorothy and Toto from going under. Within two weeks, receipts topped $40 million and *Rocky III* became the number two hit of the year, beaten only by a polyurethane puppet named ET. The film's box-office performance represented a new phenomenon. It was the first sequel in the history of the movies to make more than the original, 20 per cent more, grossing $123 million in the US alone.

The critics, who typically savage sequels because they capitalise on past success rather than take new artistic risks, dropped their prejudices and gave Stallone the best reviews of his career since Rocky stepped into the ring in 1976. They liked the macho champ playing vulnerable, and *Time* magazine paid the star perhaps the highest compliment by praising Stallone for revealing so much of himself on screen rather than hiding behind a fictional character. *Time* said he had put 'satin trunks on his autobiography'.

The box-office also got a boost from the movie's hit song, 'Eye of the Tiger', which clawed its way to the top of the pop charts and served as a free commercial for the film every time it aired on the radio. With *Rocky III*, Stallone also showed he was something of a rock impresario, having discovered Survivor, the struggling group which composed and performed 'Eye of the Tiger' on the soundtrack. The star had overheard a tape of the group playing in a colleague's office. Told that the band was having trouble getting off the ground, Stallone sent Survivor a videotape of *Rocky III* and asked them to compose a song. Three days later, he found himself humming along with one of the catchiest confections ever composed for a movie.

Despite the critical and public success, a Stallone film wouldn't have been a Stallone film without *some* controversy rearing its ugly Hydra heads. This time, it was the star's generosity that caused a brouhaha when he offered to donate the film's sculpture of Rocky Balboa to the Philadelphia Art Museum. In the first two films, Stallone ran up the museum's 68 steps arms raised in triumph. The moment became iconic, and in *Rocky III*, a sculpture commemorating it is donated to the city, where it stands at the top of the museum steps. That was in the film. When Stallone decided to let life imitate his art and donate the $60,000 statue by renowned sculptor A. Thomas Schomberg, the City Fathers thought the gift was a publicity stunt, considered the statue kitsch, and told Stallone to take it back. The sculpture ended up unceremoniously lashed to a tree in the backyard of his Malibu home until *other* residents of the City of Brotherly Love mounted a drive to get their 'Rocky' back. A compromise was achieved. Schomberg's statue ended up in front of Philadelphia's Spectrum, a hockey, basketball and boxing venue. Embarrassed by the backlash against its good taste, the city's Art Commission allowed the sculpture to remain in front of the art museum during the first two months of *Rocky III*'s release, earning the film publicity which it didn't really need.

The movie's success would have made a less self-demanding artist delighted. But the actor had always been a risk-taker, whether it was turning down big bucks for the rights to *Rocky* or getting hit in the face by a soccer ball. There was always the nagging voice whispering in his ear as he read the weekly box-office report on *Rocky III*. The public, it seemed, would only accept him when he wore boxing gloves. Put a soccer ball in his hand or a cop's badge on his chest, and movie-goers stayed away. *Rocky III* proved he wasn't a one-hit wonder, but would he remain a one-role marvel?

His next film would show Stallone remained the same gambler who had earlier risked life, limb and the rent money for a role.

Sometimes success breeds complacency. Success bored Stallone. He wanted to stretch, and not the kind you do before a heavy workout. His next role would show a superhuman elasticity on his part. It represented the biggest risk of his career since achieving stardom. It would also confirm his belief in taking risks. His choice would launch a whole new career, film series and lead to even greater success than Rocky Balboa – or Sylvester Stallone – had experienced so far.

# Chapter Nine

# A Very Cold Warrior

It wasn't the box-office success of *Rocky III* that gave Stallone the courage and confidence to take on the role of John Rambo. The script for *First Blood* came to him before the third *Rocky*'s release showed that he remained a contenduh.

Based on a novel by David Morell published in 1972, *First Blood* was an idea whose time had yet to come when it was published. The anti-hero of *First Blood*, John Rambo, is a Vietnam vet who has trouble adjusting to civilian life. Abused by the police, he goes on a killing spree. In 1972, American involvement in Vietnam was winding down amid ugly accusations about the first war America had lost. Lionised today, Vietnam vets at the time were considered dupes or collaborationists in a war without goals – or more importantly, victory. Amazingly, Warner Bros bought the rights to the novel anyway, but wiser heads kept it on the shelf for the next ten years while the old enmities and divisions eventually turned into rose-coloured nostalgia. That's when two unknown producers whose names would become synonymous with blockbuster, then bankruptcy, brought a script based on *First Blood* to *the* hottest actor in Hollywood. Displaying the *chutzpah* that would make them the hottest producers in Hollywood for a while, Andrew Vajna and Mario Kassar, with no producer credits, bought the screen rights to *First Blood* from Warners and offered the lead to Stallone.

True, they sweetened the offer to star with a then whopping pay cheque of $3.5 million, but at this point in his career and bank account, money wasn't an inducement to the risk-taking/seeking superstar. Another offer proved more attractive. Stallone didn't want to direct, but he could remould the psychotic Vietnam vet into an unequivocal hero.

Whatever the critics said of his writing efforts, Stallone viscerally knew Americans loved an underdog who turns into a Rottweiler for the sake of a good cause. Eventually, he would realise it didn't matter how high the body count rose on screen as long as the bodies belonged to the bad guys who had been done in by a super good guy. *Rocky* did it with his fists. John Rambo would do it in three films with almost every weapon known to man and a few invented by special-effects wizards. (Dynamite-tipped arrows?) By the time Stallone got finished with Morell's original Rambo, the psycho had gotten a psychic facelift as dramatic as the cosmetic surgery that had turned Rocky Balboa into Rudolph Valentino.

The new, improved Rambo is an ex-Green Beret whose heroism has earned him the Congressional Medal of Honour and the ungrateful indifference of a nation – the quintessential Vietnam veteran experience until Ronald Reagan and others became historical revisionists.

The new Rambo wasn't psycho, but he did suffer occasional bouts of post-traumatic stress syndrome. When he's arrested for vagrancy in a small town, the sheriff decides to give him a prison haircut with a switchblade. This brings to mind similar run-ins with the Viet Cong, and Rambo thinks he's back in Vietnam. In such a setting, his behaviour would be appropriate, but he's still in the middle of Middle America. Escaping from jail, he goes on a one-man, well, 'wounding' spree. One of Stallone's ingenious script changes had Rambo shooting adversaries in the leg instead of the heart. *Terminator II* employed the same trick so Arnold Schwarzenegger wouldn't be seen killing cops, just knee-capping them.

Brian Dennehy played the bull-necked Police Chief Teasle who goes a-huntin' Rambo. Kirk Douglas was hired to play Rambo's ex-commander in Vietnam, Colonel Sam Trautman, brought to town when local law enforcement proves no match for the better skilled war vet. His old commander would talk him down from the mountains and back to jail. Douglas, however, retreated after less than three days on the set. In the shooting script, his role was not much more than a cameo. He signed on with the proviso that Trautman's participation would get beefed up. Soon, Douglas found himself asking, 'Where's the beef?' It wasn't in the re-written script, and soon Douglas wasn't in the film.

The press in a knee-jerk overreaction blamed Stallone for Douglas's departure, an inaccurate accusation since the actor had been a personal hero as the star of one of Stallone's favourite fight films, 1949's *Champion*. (The younger actor had also admired Douglas's muscles a decade later in *The Vikings*.) No one believed Stallone when he insisted, 'I'm sorry Kirk Douglas left the film. He was one of my childhood heroes, and I was looking forward to working with him. His leaving had nothing to do with me.'

A lesser star but an equal talent, the genial Richard Crenna, stepped into the breach and got a gig that guaranteed him employment into the twenty-first century, a lucrative annuity that may now make Douglas wish he had accepted the cameo at face value.

Douglas's departure was only the first of many mishaps that made the shoot in Canada's British Columbia seem jinxed. Shot between November 1981 and January 1982 during one of the coldest winters in Canadian history, the freezing temperatures were the least of the production's problems. Stallone must have felt like the punching bag of movie stars as stunts gone wrong sent him to the hospital three times. The final tally: four broken ribs, third-degree burns when bullets exploded in one hand, a knifewound in the other hand, a cracked vertebra and a pulled back muscle. And all that was even though this time he used a stunt double for the more dangerous shots. Other actors also suffered. Brian Dennehy cut his hand during a knifefight with Stallone and cracked three ribs when he fell through a glass roof during another battle. A stuntman also crushed his vertebrae during a car-crash sequence.

Perhaps more frightening was the unsolved theft of $50,000 worth of guns used in the film. It was apparently an inside job since there were no signs of forced entry. The director, Ted Kotcheff, speculated on the ultimate destination of these weapons without naming the suspected culprits and incurring their wrath. 'The operation was perfect and all the guns are probably on their way to Northern Ireland or Lebanon,' Kotcheff said.

Despite the calamities, the film only went three days over schedule and kept to its relatively small budget of $16 million, an impressive economy considering the expensiveness of outdoor shooting, stunts and special effects.

Amazingly, *First Blood* had trouble finding a distributor despite the proven value of its star. The terms the novice producers demanded, however, made the movie a hard sell, not its quality. Kassar and Vajna knew the ancillary fortune the *Rocky* movies had made with TV sales, and insisted on selling only the theatrical rights to their début project. Universal, Warner Bros and Paramount refused *First Blood* under those terms, and executives at those studios must have regretted their decision as *First Blood* and its sequels turned into a franchise more lucrative than the dizzying *Rocky*s! The studios' reluctance also stemmed from the dismal track record of Stallone's non-*Rocky* films.

The orphan ended up at Orion, a new company whose founder, Mike Medavoy, had been in charge at United Artists when a no-name actor demanded the lead in a script he had written about a Philadelphia *palooka*. Medavoy not only settled for theatrical rights, but he pledged a major marketing campaign of $5 million. It turned out to be money ingeniously spent.

*First Blood* opened in November 1982 and grossed $20 million during its first month alone, with a final worldwide tally of $100 million. The success had special sweetness for Stallone. Long accused of being an artistic meddler, he not only rewrote John Rambo's character to make him less psychotic and more viewer-friendly, he also earned a co-writing credit. With *First Blood*, he proved he could succeed as both a writer and an actor without donning boxing gloves.

*Rocky III* was still playing in theatres when *First Blood* stole some of its box-office. With two huge hits out in the same year, Stallone wasn't hot, he was thermonuclear. And yet, even he had trouble getting pet projects off the ground while fighting studios and his own fear of failure.

Bankable beyond belief, Stallone was stunned when he failed to find a taker for a script he had written called *Pals*. The comedy was a younger, more macho version of *The Odd Couple*, based on the starving actor days of Marlon Brando and Wally Cox, who roomed together in New York City in the late '40s. Stallone planned to play Brando and hoped to cast an *Über*-nerd like Woody Allen or Dustin Hoffman in the role of Cox (US TV's *Mr Peepers*). Stallone essaying light comedy with a dweeb instead of a machine-gun as co-star was a scarier concept than Rocky Balboa without boxing gloves, and the script settled into development limbo. A much better fit, the title role in his script *The Bodyguard*, also got the thumbs down, way down, from every studio. Didn't these executives read the trades' box-office reports?

In a rare moment of self-doubt, Stallone considered, then passed on, a TV version of *A Streetcar Named Desire*, with *guess who* playing the role made indelible by Brando. Too indelible in Stallone's mind. 'It's a haunted play, and there was no way I could win. Everybody would compare my Stanley Kowalski with Marlon Brando's. I felt it would become a race – the 100-yard thespian "dash". Who will win, Brando's spectre or Stallone?' (This was the same man who also admitted he fell asleep watching *On the Waterfront*.)

The nastiest competition at this time, however, involved an even more quixotic industry figure than Stallone, superproducer Robert Evans. During his days as Paramount's production head, Evans had midwifed such classics as *Chinatown* and a pair of *Godfather*s. Going solo, he became the Tiffany's of independent producers with a gilt-edged collection of scripts with directors attached. Evans brought a camera-ready project, *The Cotton Club*, to Stallone, who signed on immediately without making the usual script rewriting demands. It was a wise decision, since the screenwriter was *The Godfather*'s Mario

Puzo, writing about what he knew best, gangsters of the past. Francis Coppola would direct the film about the famous Harlem nightclub that showcased black talent for white audiences during the 1920s.

The deal fell apart but not for the usual artistic differences. This time it was mostly about ego in general, producing in particular. Stallone had hired a new manager, Jerry Weintraub, and demanded his manager receive a producing credit on the film. Evans, who considered himself the production equivalent of an author, balked. Stallone walked.

(More than a decade later, Stallone suggested the real reason he left the project, and it had nothing to do with a producing credit. In the October 1995 issue of *Movieline* magazine, the actor said that during pre-production, Evans showed him obscene photographs of himself and a near underaged girl. They were old snapshots of the woman Stallone was romantically involved with at the time. 'He brought out lewd pictures of this girl, taken ten years earlier – I mean really lewd – showed them and said, "Don't you think that's funny?" I told him, "Showing me pornography of a girl I'm dating is going to endear you to me?" That's when I washed my hands of him and pulled out of *The Cotton Club*. I was like, "How dare this guy show me pictures of this girl in a compromising situation with him when she was 18 years old?" I realised he was demented, but he blames me, I guess, for having had to go out and get someone else to star in his movie.')

Evans got Richard Gere to star, and the overbudgeted production almost destroyed Paramount. Stallone escaped looking sharp. The careers of Coppola and Evans would spiral downward for the rest of the decade and into the next. Evans added another nail to his career coffin by going public big time against Stallone, ignoring the cardinal rule of the care and feeding of box-office behemoths: 'Stab your enemies in the back, not the front. You may need to work with them in the future.' Evans made public a letter he had written before *First Blood*'s receipts revealed its success: Stallone, Evans said before John Rambo assaulted movie theatres, had failed 'to prove [himself] outside the ring. I hope Mr Weintraub will find you that magic property that will elevate you to be a *bona fide* star without having to wear boxing gloves.' If there's something like the opposite of wish-fulfilment, Evans's hope turned out to be prophetic when only two months later *First Blood* proved the star had found just that project.

There would be more.

# Chapter Ten

# Italian Stallions

*The Cotton Club* had been only one part of a long-term deal Stallone negotiated at Paramount, where he set up an office. He also used the back lot as a jogging field, which caused more employee 'problems' for the studio. At the same time every day, Stallone did a few laps around the studio, during which time work came to a halt as everyone from secretaries to top executives left their desks to gawk at the muscular superstar trotting past their windows. Apprised of the work stoppage, Stallone graciously agreed to vary his jogging times, and Paramount returned to full productivity.

Strangely, the studio was not so co-operative with its new track star in residence. It flat out refused to hire Frank Sr as a script-reader, the lowest level of employment on the production pecking order except for gofer. A psychotherapist might offer a fistful of reasons why Stallone did not protest the studio's refusal to put his whistling dad on the payroll.

Paramount delightedly deferred to another hiring idea.

The studio had been begging John Travolta since 1977 to reprise the role of Tony Manero in *Saturday Night Fever*. Unlike Stallone at the time, Travolta was something less than hot. His star hadn't fizzled, but none of his follow-up films except *Grease* had generated *Fever*'s heat. On-screen pairings with leading ladies like Olivia Newton-John in *Two of a Kind* and Lily Tomlin in *Moment by Moment* lacked sexual chemistry, the reasons for which we will leave to the tabloids and their well-paid libel lawyers.

Travolta needed a hit, but he feared sequelitis more than box-office poison. All the proposed scripts for *Saturday Night Fever II* failed to woo him until he fell in love with *Rocky III*. Stallone proved that a sequel (even a second time around) could stay true to the original and, better yet, make even more money. After a screening of the third *Rocky*, Travolta told the men in suits at Paramount, 'If we can just get the energy into *Staying Alive* [*Fever II*'s title], we'll have a hit.' All it took was a single intra-studio phone call to that other handsome Italian on the back lot, and the deal was set up over the weekend. On Monday morning, it made the front page of the *Los Angeles Times* entertainment section, although it helped that Travolta had called on Saturday night to inform the reporter who wrote the breathless cover piece.

Stallone agreed to direct and 'volunteered' to rewrite the script, which he promptly dumped. Travolta was happy to help carry out the trash, since the script had Manero give up his dancing aspirations and become a community activist. 'The first script was anti-dance. Tony wanted to go to block parties in Manhattan and social counselling, getting the neighbourhoods together . . . the one thing I know the audience wants is for him to keep dancing. His appeal is as a tough guy who gets away with dancing,' Travolta said.

There were no artistic differences between the actor and his new director-co-writer. Stallone wanted to do *Rocky* in a leotard, and that's the script he wrote. If Balboa could go from incompetent loan shark employee to heavyweight champion of the world, Manero could make a similar leap from a smoky Brooklyn disco to Broadway. Stallone cloned Rocky and added kicks to the hand movements.

Early drafts of Stallone's re-write must have terrified Paramount executives, who probably anaesthetised themselves by re-reading *First Blood*'s box-office figures. In one version, Tony Manero triumphs on the Great White Way in a musical remake of *The Odyssey*! Stallone discarded that idea because he feared the general audience was unfamiliar with Homer. So he cast Manero in a musical remake of *Paradise Lost*, called *Satan's Alley*.

Unlike *Rocky III*, *Saturday Night Fever II* would be autobiographical. Stallone's autobiography, not Travolta's. In real life, Stallone had left his wife for a glamorous starlet. In the film, Manero dumps his dumpy girlfriend and falls for the lithe co-star of *Satan's Alley*. Publicly, Stallone hedged on whether he had written a screenplay *à clef* based on the Sylvester-Sasha-Susan Anton triangle. 'I guess it was subliminal, but it's true. I am drawing on past experience.'

The star has more than once said he never tried traditional psychotherapy because he found his work, especially writing, very therapeutic. He must have been glad to be in the middle of re-writes on *Staying Alive* because he needed a lot of 'self-counselling' when a personal tragedy occurred in his perfect life.

# Chapter Eleven

# The Sad Case of Seargeoh Stallone

In September 1982, Stallone's three-year-old younger son, Seargeoh, was diagnosed with autism, a brain disorder whose victims suffer extreme detachment from others and their own lives.

Stallone and his wife were seated in the sunny living-room of their Pacific Palisades mansion overlooking the ocean when Dr Edward Ritvo of UCLA's Department of Child Pyschiatry told the shocked parents the results of a two-month-long series of tests administered to Seargeoh at the UCLA Medical Center.

The puzzled couple had brought their beautiful blond younger son in for testing because his behaviour had become progressively troubling. After a birth with no complications, which Stallone watched in a mirror in the delivery room, Seargeoh seemed like a perfect child. 'He's a beautiful baby,' the father whispered to the mother as he checked out the newborn to make sure all toes and fingers were accounted for. Unlike their first son, Sage, who had his father's Italian colouring, Seargeoh took after his Czech mom. 'Now we've got one that's dark and one that's blond,' the proud father said.

Seargeoh's physical development early on didn't raise any red flags. In fact, his precocity suggested he might follow in his father's athletic footsteps. By six months, he was crawling all over the 30,000-square-foot mansion. At eight months, he sat up. Three months later, like Rocky Balboa at the end of his first fight, Seargeoh could stand up.

His mental progress presented a more complicated picture. Seargeoh knew the alphabet at 18 months and could count to 75, another stunning feat of precocity. He was a wiz at reading flashcards with words like 'dog', 'cat', 'run', 'up' and 'down'. His conversational skills didn't match his other verbal skills, however. 'As far as talking with you goes,' Sasha said, 'he could not do that. So we thought we had a young genius who was the strong, silent type. He just appeared very shy.'

One problem broke his father's heart. Seargeoh could point to photographs of Stallone and say, 'Daddy'. When the real thing said, 'Who am I?', Seargeoh ignored his father.

The child began to demonstrate other worrying symptoms. He didn't make eye contact and refused to play with other kids. Like his father, he displayed symptoms of hyperactivity and penny-ante versions of his father's own juvenile delinquency like scrawling graffiti on walls.

By the age of two and a half, Seargeoh's behaviour had become so upsetting, his anxious parents took him to a series of paediatricians who insisted that the child was just going through a phase which he would grow out of.

No. Seargeoh's 'terrible twos' didn't end on his third birthday. By then, his parents feared their son had severe psychological problems and, typically, blamed themselves. Sasha said, 'We felt possibly we were forcing him a little too much to talk, because when we urged him to talk more, he retreated even further. I kept thinking: He's angry at us because we want something from him and he's not ready to do it yet.'

After the tests at UCLA, not only Dr Ritvo but his colleague, Dr Betty Jo Freeman, a clinical psychologist, made a 'mansion-call' with the bad news. 'This is a hard thing to tell you,' Ritvo said to the couple. 'Your son has autism.'

Ritvo recalled their reaction. 'When I told the Stallones what we had found, it was as if I had rolled a truck over them. At three and a half, Seargeoh had the psychological development of a 16-month-old child.' What they had suspected was a brooding 'genius' turned out to be one of 10,000 children diagnosed with autism every year in the US.

The panicky Stallones peppered the medical team with questions, trying to find some hope in what they soon found out was a hopeless prognosis for their son. What would happen to Seargeoh as he grew older? Would he eventually relate to peers, drive a car, make a living, go on dates, get married?

Sasha said, 'To everything we asked, the answer was "no". Dr Ritvo told us that if autistic children develop to a certain stage, they can do simple things like weight lifting.' Although a gym-aholic himself, Stallone did not find this news comforting.

Ritvo also told them that if they were lucky, Seargeoh might be able to perform simple tasks like cleaning the house and doing odd jobs, something the offspring of a multimillionaire would never need to do.

The doctors' parting advice left the couple devastated. Dr Ritvo told them that when autistic children reach their teens, the parents often have to do the unthinkable. 'Most parents put them in homes because it's too draining to keep them at home. That way they can get special schooling. Otherwise, you have to have a live-in therapist,' the UCLA professor said.

Sasha began to cry: 'I can't have it!' Stallone went into Rocky-mode, although the optimism that had helped him overcome obstacles throughout his life just wouldn't work in this, his greatest challenge. 'We'll do something!' he told his wife. 'He'll pull through!'

Stallone had battled handicaps since birth. He projected his own success on to his son. Later, he and his wife went into the nursery where Seargeoh slept, seemingly at peace. Stallone pulled the blanket over his son and whispered in his ear, 'Heal yourself, Seargeoh. You can do it!'

They wondered why they were being punished. Had they done something to deserve their son's illness? Sasha speculated, 'It was as if somebody said, "You've gotten this far, you've been this successful. But where is your next goal? Why don't you try this one on for size?"'

The first thing they both ruled out was institutionalising their son. Then they decided to fight back. Actually, Sasha would play Rambo in the fight. Her husband, busy directing *Staying Alive*, would provide emotional support and money to wage the war.

Sasha never suspected Seargeoh had autism. Documentaries on the disorder showed children with much worse behavioural problems than Seargeoh's crayon 'murals' and conversational shortcomings. She decided to become an amateur expert and researched the disease. Just as her husband used food to define a new movie role, she took Seargeoh to a nutritionist, who recommended megadoses of vitamins and a change in diet. The results were dramatic and quick. Within four days, Seargeoh's hyperactivity diminished and he began to make eye contact.

During her research, Sasha came across a series of books by Barry Neil Kaufman, who 'cured' his son's autism with a therapy he created called 'Option Process'. Now a teenager, his son, Kaufman claimed, attended public school and earned good grades.

Stallone put down the script he was re-writing for Travolta and flew to New York with Sasha for a meeting with Kaufman. The couple became disciples and students. They spent 12-hour days learning Kaufman's therapy. Option Process takes a *laissez-faire* approach to the autistic's development. Before, the Stallones had pushed their son to come out of his shell. Kaufman recommended that Seargeoh be allowed to progress at his own rate, with acceptance rather than with pressure, however well intentioned. In fact, parents are encouraged to imitate their child's behaviour. If he rocks back and forth, a common symptom, do the same thing until he's gained your trust and feels your acceptance. Gradually, get the child to imitate your behaviour, Kaufman said.

Developmental pyschologists have not given Kaufman's theories their imprimatur. Dr Bernard Rimland, the parent of an autistic child and founder of the National Society for Children and Adults with Autism and the Institute for Child Behaviour Research in San Diego, California, felt sceptical about Option Process, but didn't dismiss the procedure out of hand, counselling more research. And besides, the other options offered even less hope.

Back in Los Angeles, Sasha assembled a battle team with five friends and therapists for troops. Each of them spent three-hour shifts with Seargeoh. He was constantly engaged but not pressured as they chatted, sang, played and read to him. UCLA's Dr Ritvo also treated Seargeoh as traditional backup in case Kaufman turned out to be a fraud.

So far, Sasha remains a disciple, not a sceptic. After only three months practising Kaufman's theories, Seargeoh leapt from the developmental age of a 16-month-old to his chronological age, three! In 1983, a year after his diagnosis, Sasha told *McCall's* magazine, 'I'll put an apple on the counter. He'll see it and want it. He knows how to say apple, so we've taught him to say, "I want." I encourage him to talk by saying, "What do you want?' When he says, 'Want apple." I tell him, "Say, I want apple." And when he does that, I say, "Good boy. You can have it." Then I ask, "Can I have a bite?" He gives me a bite, and so that way he learns communicative speech.'

Sadly, cut to two years later to the cover of *People* magazine, which displayed Stallone in Rocky's boxing trunks triumphantly holding Seargeoh. Inside, however, the picture was different. 'There is no real father-and-son thing there. I have to become his playmate. With a child like this, you have to put away your ego. You can't force him into your world. I sort of go along with whatever he is doing. Sometimes he likes to draw, mostly abstract things, and he has puzzles that we work on together. After he gets to the point where he trusts you, a little more communication can start.'

Stallone tried to sound hopeful, but in contrast to his initial Rocky-Rambo reaction to the diagnosis, his perspective three years later reflected a combination of resignation and diminished expectations. 'To have a child in this predicament is extremely sad,' he said in 1985. 'It's almost like a radio station – he fades on and off of the signal.'

Still a proud father, he boasted of his son's progress and told himself things could be worse. 'He can pretty much feed himself now. Many autistic children are violent, Seargeoh is not. We're lucky. A brain scan showed there was no deterioration of the brain. So there is a chance that he could recover.'

While Sasha provided day-to-day attention, her busy husband helped in his own way, which also benefited Seargeoh's fellow-sufferers. Every première for the actor's films became a fundraiser for the Stallone Foundation for Autism Research and related charities.

Sasha sounded more like Rocky than Rocky. 'Until we learned of Seargeoh's autism, I guess you could say that Sly and I were living pretty selfish lives. We led our separate, busy lives . . . Now we're working for a goal, to help find a cure for autism.'

His wife put her promising photography career on hold to become a full-time carer and fundraiser. Her husband became even more of a workaholic. In the 15 years since the diagnosis, Stallone has starred in (and often written and directed) more than 20 films.

While Sasha stayed home with Seargeoh, he reported to the back lot to continue work on *Staying Alive*. He was a workaholic, but not a glutton. The one hat he refused to wear when *Staying Alive* went into production was that of co-star. Officially, Stallone refused the studio's request to appear on screen. He said he didn't want to upstage the star. Privately, Paramount refused to put its money where its mouth already was, kissing the star's butt. Travolta got $2 million to reprise Manero, Stallone earned $1 million for directing and rewriting. For a mere $2 million more, he told the studio, he would be happy to upstage Travolta. With the budget already at $18 million, Paramount reluctantly kept Stallone in the director's chair and at his writer's desk. Stallone also realised that if the costly project failed, he'd take the fall. If it flew, it would be Travolta's vehicle. (Stallone, however, couldn't resist a shy homage to Hitchcock with a micro-cameo where he bumps into Travolta on the street and glares at him.)

Although Paramount had balked at hiring Frank Sr the studio gave Frank Jr a gig writing songs and a bit part. One of Frank's singles, 'Far From Over', made the pop charts, although the title song was reserved for the first film's composers-performers, The Bee Gees.

Just as he reconceived the original script, Stallone decided to reconstruct Travolta's body. Prior to filming, the lean stud from

*Saturday Night Fever* hadn't hit the gym for a year. Kinder people described him as 'puffy'. Stallone declared his protégé 20 pounds overweight.

The director had transformed his own fleshy physique into something close to a competitive bodybuilder's for *Rocky III* and inexplicably felt much of that film's success was due to his pumped pecs rather than his script or direction. If 18-inch biceps could lead to a $100 million-plus box-office, maybe a Rocky-like regimen could pump up *Staying Alive*'s ticket sales if Travolta pumped up his body.

Another transformation took place at this time, which only observant fans of the first *Fever* would notice. Stallone converted his charge to a weird rite of competitive bodybuilders. He shaved his chest, something Stallone himself had been doing unnoticed for years. If you look closely at the first *Rocky*, the star has a tuft of chest hair. By *Rocky III*, he's what pro bodybuilders call 'smooth', i.e. hairless. In *Saturday Night Fever*, Travolta has an iconic sequence in front of the mirror wearing only underpants and displaying a torso as hirsute as Tom Selleck's. In the sequel, he looks like product placement for Epilady or Nair.

Bodybuilders shave so the hair doesn't hide the muscles they have worked so hard to develop. Not only is Travolta's chest a hair-free zone during the movie, much of the time he seems to be oiled up like a Mr America contestant posing on stage, muscles glistening for extra effect. The morning shave was nothing compared to what Stallone had planned for the rest of the day at the gym, where they sometimes spent up to 14 hours pumping.

When they weren't in the gym, you were likely to find them dining together, but not just for social reasons. Travolta loved to eat, and his coach attended every meal to make sure he didn't stray from his diet. A reluctant weight-watcher, Travolta said he fantasised about chocolate cake all the time. After a few months, looking in the mirror made him forget about eating dessert. Eventually, he became a convert and went on to write a diet and workout book of his own, *Staying Fit*. In it, he promised to keep the 20 pounds off permanently. Over the years, moviegoers saw dramatic proof he eventually reneged on his promise.

Stallone crowed like a personal trainer, 'If John keeps it up, I'll have to fight him in *Rocky IV*.' He was kidding, of course, but after he made the suggestion, you can imagine phone calls flying back and forth between *Rocky*'s home, United Artists, and *Staying Alive*'s, Paramount, for discussions about just such a pairing in the fourth *Rocky*.

*Staying Alive* opened in July 1983 with respectable but not blockbuster business, earning 60 per cent of the original, for a total gross of $64 million in the US. The reviews were dismissive but not disastrous. Travolta revived his career with a modest hit and got a great new body as part of the deal. Stallone proved he could turn in a professional product, imposing his will on a complicated production without imposing his mug all over the screen.

Paramount was pleased enough to continue its partnership with Stallone and inundated him with scripts. The studio threw everything but the phone book at their in-house superstar. And when we say *everything*, that's not an exaggeration. Perhaps the looniest idea was also the one that came closest to production. Paramount asked Stallone to write, direct and star in *The Godfather, Part III*, playing the son of Michael Corleone, Al Pacino in the previous *Godfather*s. Also on the studio's delusional wish list was Travolta as Stallone's son!

Today, and even back then, the first two *Godfather* films are considered twentieth century classics. To hand over the reins of the third installment to the maker of popcorn classics horrified a cabal of Young Turks at Paramount who quietly worked to subvert the deal. Their motivation to kill the Stallone project grew when they learned that his script would turn the Corleone family of gangsters into heroes battling corrupt cops.

A dissident group of Paramount executives made overtures to Coppola and Pacino to save the *Godfather* franchise and made sure that Stallone found out about this double-dealing. The ploy worked. Although an agreement with the star was all but final, including a $5 million fee upfront for triple duty on *The Godfather III*, when he learned of the counter-offer to Coppola

& Co, Stallone walked off the project. While the in-house rebels at the studio prevented sacrilege, they only served as spoilers. The Coppola version went into development limbo for seven years, before being revived in 1990.

Undaunted, the studio tried to keep Stallone on the back lot with another script that had been rejected by Mickey Rourke. The studio didn't blush at offering their biggest star sloppy seconds, because the screenplay was a terrific vehicle for an action star. The hero, a tough street cop in the East, goes to Southern California to track down the killers of his best friend. Stallone liked the concept, but he demanded a re-write – by him.

The original script had been a cop caper, the violence tempered with lots of wisecracks. Stallone's re-write shocked Paramount and the producers of the film, superstars in their own right, Don Simpson and Jerry Bruckheimer. Stallone turned the glib hero into the strong silent type, the type who uses Uzis instead of wit to disarm opponents. Actually, he kills them. As rewritten, the climactic shootout piled up more bodies than *Hamlet*'s finale. Don Simpson said diplomatically of the star's draft, 'He did a marvellous job . . . but it wasn't comedic enough.'

The studio hired another re-write guy, who turned the action into a comedy caper, which was then offered to a supernovaing new star by the name of Eddie Murphy. The film became the number one box-office hit of 1984, a wide-awake sleeper called *Beverly Hills Cop*.

Inexplicably, Stallone had cut the humour out of his re-write, but chose another even broader comedy for his next film. Instead of playing Axel Foley in *Beverly Hills Cop*, he decided to play a singing cab driver opposite Dolly Parton in *the* biggest embarrassment of his career, *Rhinestone*.

Parton plays a country and western singer who performs at a New York City club. She makes a bet with the owner (Ron Leibman) that she can turn the first guy she sees into a successful singer. If she wins, the bar owner will let her out of her contract and move on. If she loses, she has to stay at the downscale venue – plus, have sex with the boss.

After the bet is made, Stallone pulls up driving his cab, and Parton really has her work cut out for her. Years later, when I interviewed Stallone for *People* magazine, he jokingly claimed he thought his agent said '*urban* cowboy, not '*rhinestone* cowboy,' when the concept was explained to him.

Executives at Twentieth Century Fox, which lured Stallone away from Paramount for the musical, had anxiety attacks as they watched the dailies. Part of the joke was supposed to be that Stallone's cabbie couldn't sing. But the heart-warming Pygmalion gimmick was that eventually Dolly would transform him into a rootin', tootin' rhinestone cowboy who *could* sing. As they say, 'only in the movies . . .' when describing an improbable fantasy on screen. Not *this* movie. Serious thought was given to dubbing Stallone's voice as the dailies sounded more and more like a screeching cat doing a duet with, well, the Grammy-winning Parton. Timid executives rejected the idea, fearing it would alienate the star. And some even thought it would be funny and draw the curious who wanted to hear just how badly Stallone sang.

Curiosity wasn't a big enough draw, and *Rhinestone* flopped in the summer of 1984 with a final domestic gross of $12 million, half its budget, which included $8 million for the two stars and the monstrous expense of shutting down major New York streets for Stallone to ride a horse down.

As an entertainment reporter for UPI in 1984, I received an invitation to the movie première, which strangely was held at the Picwood, a downscale theatre in a blue-collar neighbourhood on Pico Boulevard in West Los Angeles. Premières are typically filled with friends of the cast and crew, along with nervous executives and agents of the stars. No matter how bad a film is, the audience at these galas has an ulterior motive to root for the movie.

Unlike every other première I had attended in my career as a journalist, no one applauded during the credits. The faulty air-conditioning in the sweltering theatre didn't improve the mood either. A lavish fundraiser for the Stallones' autism foundation took place a few blocks east of the theatre on the back lot at Fox. Several soundstages had been magnificently decorated with the standard Lucullan buffet. But the party resembled a wake since the revellers had already seen the 'corpse' on screen.

I witnessed a telling incident at the party which suggested why Stallone has such a complicated public image. When I interviewed him for *People* magazine, I was struck by his wit and charm. His articulateness, which almost every other interviewer has commented on with surprise, contrasted with the monosyllabic Neanderthals he played on screen. Was this the same guy, I wondered, who threatened to punch out a movie critic who had recommended verbal castration after *Paradise Alley* came out?

The *other* Stallone, however, was on display at the post-première wake. As the star and a giant bodyguard ascended a narrow staircase on the soundstage, a fan approached with a velvet painting he had done of Rocky Balboa. A temperamental superstar might have been appalled at being turned into the boxing equivalent of an Elvis on velvet painting, but Stallone graciously consented to autograph the monstrosity at the fan's request.

However, while he took his time trying to write on velvet with a fountain pen, his bodyguard shoved his arm against the wall and refused to let the other people on the crowded staircase, including me, pass by. There was enough room for two lanes of traffic, but it came to a long halt as the bodyguard literally threw his weight around. Feeling foolish, the partygoers, who had paid big bucks to attend the charity event, stood like schoolkids at a crosswalk as the bodyguard refused to let us pass until his employer finished turning the icky painting into an instant collector's item thanks to the star's signature. It was only a mildly irritating display of ego, but suggested that more dramatic stories of the star's ego run amok on movie sets could also be true.

The failure of *Rhinestone* was followed by a personal setback a few months after its release. Their son's diagnosis of autism had initially brought Sasha and her husband closer together as they attacked the disease with fundraising and caring for their son. But the common battle wasn't enough to sustain a united front. On 29 November 1984, Sasha Stallone filed for divorce. And unlike previous separations, this one stuck. The divorce became final in 1985. The split was amicable, however, even though Sasha's $32 million settlement made international headlines.

Strangely, his ex-wife didn't get the house. Mom and the two kids moved six blocks away from the Pacific Palisades mansion. Stallone got unlimited visitation rights, and between films spent two to three days a week with his sons. On weekends, he took the kids to the Malibu beach house.

As an antidote to personal and professional setbacks, Stallone threw himself into his next project, which began as usual with a major re-write by the star. This took special *chutzpah*, since he was tinkering with the work of a major writer-director, James Cameron. Cameron didn't object, explaining, 'This script has no redeeming moral value.' And he was describing *his* draft, not Stallone's!

# Chapter Twelve

# Bodycounts and Box-Office

Maybe Cameron, who had recently turned Arnold Schwarzenegger into a contender with *The Terminator*, didn't mind being re-written because *a*: Stallone was actually the originator of the character Cameron provided dialogue for, and *b*: Cameron wouldn't be directing the film, a sequel to *First Blood*, which became far better known as *Rambo*.

If the audience didn't want Stallone stretching as a singing, wise-cracking cowboy, he would return to a guaranteed stereotype, a guy who doesn't talk and does his thinking with firearms and grenades.

The first *First Blood* had been made on a shoestring budget and on the fly in the frigid north of Canada. *Rambo: First Blood, Part II*, enjoyed triple the original's budget, a then huge $30 million, and a much warmer climate with Mexico doubling as Vietnam. In fact, after the day's shooting in the jungle, it was only a ten-minute drive to the luxury resort of Acapulco.

In 1982, John Rambo's first screen appearance represented a dicey proposition. The country was in recession, the Vietnam War had not yet been sentimentalised, and Ronald Reagan's conservatism had not been embraced because people were more worried about unemployment than political ideology. Three years later, with a booming economy and a popular Cold

Warrior in the Oval Office, the second Rambo perfectly fitted the *Zeitgeist*.

At the end of *First Blood*, John Rambo goes to jail for shooting up an entire town. The sequel opens a few years later, with Rambo breaking rocks in a prison quarry. Richard Crenna's Colonel Trautman shows up with an offer. Rambo will be pardoned and released if he undertakes a mission to Vietnam to look for PoWs still held there.

Reluctantly, Rambo agrees, even though he is told that if he finds PoWs not to rescue them. Vietnam has demanded a $4 billion ransom for their return. It's cheaper for the US to deny the existence of captive Americans and save on ransom money. Rambo is flown to Vietnam and parachutes alone into what the US government believes is a deserted POW camp. Rambo will return with photographic proof that no Americans remain in Communist hands.

When Rambo drops in, he finds half a dozen Americans penned up in a stockade. Ignoring orders, he liberates the camp and leads the PoWs to the appointed rendezvous with a US military helicopter. Rambo was supposed to show up empty-handed. When the helicopter pilot sees the PoWs, he aborts the mission and leaves the men stranded in the middle of enemy territory deep in the jungles of Vietnam.

The rest of the film involves Rambo leading his charges to safety. In between, he is captured and tortured by a Russian advisor to the Vietnamese. Rambo escapes, commandeers a Russian helicopter and flies his charges to Thailand, where he beats up the American military officer (not Crenna's Trautman) who betrayed his mission.

Typically, Stallone interpreted the role by transforming his body once again. Added muscle had pumped up *Rocky III*'s box-office, he believed, so two months before filming began on *Rambo*, he hired former Mr Olympia Franco Columbu to add even more muscle – ten pounds – to his already perfect frame. Columbu gave up all his other clients and charged a protesting Stallone a fortune. 'Why don't you just take my house?' he joked to his trainer.

The two men hit the gym twice a day, six days a week.

Stallone had ordered Columbu to train him as though the actor were prepping for the Mr Olympia contest, the top title in bodybuilding. After six weeks, Stallone's arms had gone from 16 inches to 18 inches, his chest from 44 inches to 50 inches. Already an icon, the Stallone physique became a temple of self-worship.

For a change, unlike most of his other ultra action films, Stallone suffered no injuries during the shoot, which was hellish nonetheless. Early on, a hurricane struck Acapulco and shut down production for a week. A remote house Stallone lived in near the jungle was threatened by an avalanche during the hurricane. The roads were washed away, so rather than get buried under rubble, he hiked incommunicado nine miles in the rain from his home to the film's production office.

Tragically, a special effects expert, Cliff Wenger Jr fell 200 feet to his death during the filming of a waterfall sequence. A near tragedy eerily reminiscent of *The Twilight Zone* film disaster two years earlier occurred when a helicopter crashed, narrowly missing several actors.

Despite the 100-degree temperatures and attacks by tarantulas and snakes, which weren't part of the script, Stallone's energy remained boundless. After a 12-hour shoot, he would hit the gym to keep his screen image picture perfect. Between takes, he also found time to write *Rocky IV.*

The terror and toil in retrospect seemed worth it when *Rambo* débuted in May 1985. After only three days of release, it had earned $32 million, the third highest opening ever, topped only by two Indiana Jones epics.

American action movies tend to fare better abroad, where their minimal dialogue helps breach the language barrier and *Rambo* was no exception. Two months after its release worldwide, *Rambo*'s box-office take neared a quarter billion dollars!

Macho action movies target the all-important teen audience, who turn hits into blockbusters by returning to the theatre to see the film again and again. Although *Rambo*'s wild plot attracted male teens, 40 per cent of the audience turned out to be female adults. Maybe the star's compulsive bodyshaping hadn't been so bizarre as it seemed. Were women packing the theatres to watch helicopters blasted out of the sky and see a Russian sadist slice up Stallone? Or were they going to admire his shirtless body, which got more screen time than his female co-star, Julia Nickson, who played his Vietnamese jungle guide. His apparent narcissism turned out to be an adroit marketing tool, since surveys show that women decide which movie to see, not their male dates. Stallone theorised that women in the audience didn't want to marry him; they wanted to mother him. 'It's amazing, like 82 per cent [of females] wanted to go back and see it again. Even though it's a war film, it is kind of a sensual film. The character is one of those misunderstood types that I think you can feel maternal toward, in an odd way,' he said.

The critics were unfazed by the box-office or the bod. The *Wall Street Journal* called the film, in which enemy bullets always missed Rambo, but his ammo always hit the spot, 'hare-brained'. The *New Yorker* labelled *Rambo* 'narcissistic jingoism'. And unlike the general female movie-going audience, the *Washington Post* remained singularly unimpressed by the star's pecs: 'Sly's body looks fine. Now can't you come up with a workout for the soul?'

A much more important critic, however, loved *Rambo*, and his two-thumbs up made national headlines. Before a press conference to announce the rescue of hostages hijacked during a TWA flight, President Reagan said, 'After seeing *Rambo* last night, boy, I know what to do the next time this happens.'

A politician who had been there, done that, did not agree with his Commander in Chief. Then Governor of Nebraska, Bob Kerrey, a vet who lost part of his foot fighting in Vietnam and won the Congressional Medal of Honour, condemned Stallone for playing armchair warrior. The film, Kerrey complained, 'made the [Vietnam War] look like fun'.

While Reagan loved *Rambo*, foreign policy-makers feared the film's virulent anti-Communism would aggravate East–West relations and provide more ammunition for Reagan's already frightening belligerence toward the Soviet bloc. Stallone himself was horrified that he had unintentionally become what he called the 'Jane Fonda of the Right'. 'I'm not political,' he insisted. He just wanted to honour Vietnam vets. If he made $20 million, his personal take, in the process, well, isn't America a wonderful country after all? His claims of being apolitical, however, were undercut with public pronouncements about US policy abroad. As the Reagan administration was covertly trying to overthrow Nicaragua's Marxist regime, Stallone suggested a more Rambo-like approach to ousting the Commies. 'If we're going to go into Nicaragua, we ought to be prepared to go *all* the way. Otherwise, we're going to be constantly harassed and eventually humiliated. Again . . .' he said in a national magazine, referring to the the United States' failed policy in Vietnam.

As much as it turned off critics and liberals, pronouncements like that sold tickets, and the studio used anti-Communism as a marketing tool. Stallone himself would infuse his next project with more of the same.

# Chapter Thirteen

# Cold War
# Sizzles on Screen

Like *Rambo*, *Rocky IV* took on the Russians and won. The right-wing subtext of the Vietnam epic became the text of Balboa's fourth trip to the ring and screen. For the prizefighter's nemesis this go round, he chose an even larger, more villainous opponent, a Russian heavyweight named Ivan Drago, played by Swedish actor Dolph Lundgren, best known as disco diva Grace Jones's boyfriend.

Drago has been pumped with drugs and state-of-the-art computerised training to become a contender. When he kills Carl Weathers's Apollo Creed at the beginning of the film, the rest of the story dramatises Rocky's vendetta against Drago in particular and the unfair political system – plus steroids – that have turned Drago into a killing machine.

While *Rambo* and its political philosophy reflected a collaboration between director George Cosmatos, co-screenwriter James Cameron and Stallone, the politics of *Rocky IV* belonged solely to its star, who had solo writing credit and directed the film, which was shot from March to July 1985. *Rocky IV* was also a family affair. Stallone cast his son, Sage, as Rocky Jr although the credits listed him as 'Rocky Krakoff' in an unsuccessful attempt to fool paparazzi and enquiring reporters.

In contrast to Drago's Frankenstein-like moulding inside a high-tech Russian lab, Rocky trains in the tundra of Russia. Actually, the scenes were shot in Wyoming, since the Soviet Union wasn't about to allow the world's most famous anti-Leninist to invade their turf or tundra.

Stallone's body had already been overworked at the gym, and Columbu's torturous regime continued. As part of Rocky's on-screen preparation for the fight, he pulls a 1,200-pound sled filled with rocks. While shooting the scene, the actor heard something snap, but he ignored the warning. A few weeks later, during a fight scene with Lundgren, a two-time kickboxing champ in Europe, who weighed 240 pounds and towered over Stallone at six feet six inches, Stallone began to suffer excruciating chest pains. A trip to the hospital indicated the feared heart attack was a bruised heart muscle and bleeding capillaries, caused by pulling the sled and getting pounded by Lundgren, who had rammed the star's diaphragm into his heart!

This was the most serious injury Stallone had ever sustained, but he was back on the set working both sides of the camera only ten days after the suspected heart attack. Nursing him back to health was his co-star and offscreen girlfriend, Brigitte Nielsen, who played Lundgren's wife in a microscopic cameo. Their affair began in a blaze of romantic gestures and ended a mere 18 months later in ugly recriminations that played themselves out in the international press.

The story of their romance began like an X-rated fairy tale, including pictures. Nielsen's, to be precise. Unlike a fairy tale, this one's ending was bitter.

Nielsen met Stallone when she was a 21-year-old starlet, whose first film, *Red Sonja*, a female clone of Conan the Barbarian, had completed production but had not yet been released. Nielsen had been pursuing Stallone by letter, however, since she was 11 years old after she saw the original *Rocky* in her native Denmark.

A decade later and Stallone is in New York for a 24-hour layover. Nielsen, by now a model and a (nearly) movie star, is also in town and learns that the object of her ten-year affection-obsession is staying at a hotel, the Essex House. She lay siege to Stallone by inundating him with letters. Stallone tore them up, fearing a stalker. She finally caught his attention with a follow-up letter that included her modelling photos. That was Stallone's PG-rated recollection. Nielsen told me when I interviewed her for *People* magazine that she had sent him nude pictures of herself.

She finally got his attention by 'illustrating her request' for a meeting. 'From the letters I had always pictured her three feet tall and 400 pounds, with buck-teeth and a horrendous complexion. But what I saw made my knees a little weak,' Stallone said. Stallone was so, uh, stimulated by the photos, he claims he literally ran in the pouring rain two blocks to her hotel because he couldn't find a taxi.

When she came to the door, his knees got weaker. 'I pounded on her door, and when it opened I saw this wonderful vision. She's so imposing when she comes in. She had the flaming red hair from *Red Sonja*, and she looked extraordinary.' Stallone planned to stay 15 minutes, he said. They spent four hours together that night. They were inseparable for the next year and a half.

Nielsen was six feet tall and very, well, buxom. *Vanity Fair* called her 'the freakishly beautiful Brigitte Nielsen'. Like all legendary romances, this one has contradictory versions. According to one magazine, Nielsen shoved a glossy of herself under his hotel room door, with the inscription: 'My name is Brigitte Nielsen. I'd really like to meet you. Here's my number.' Stallone called, then came over. His first words: 'I've got to get to know you better.'

A few months after they met, Nielsen became famous, not because of *Red Sonja*, which came and went in the summer of 1985, but for being the consort of Hollywood's number one star. Although Nielsen only had *Sonja* on her list of film credits, she had Stallone on her arm. It was enough of a connection for *People* magazine to send a reporter, me, in pursuit of the elusive Nielsen for a major story on a minor star with big connections.

After negotiations with her publicist that had the complexity of a SALT treaty and repeated cancellations, I finally sat down with Nielsen in an office on the back lot of MGM (now Sony). Despite her age, she was amazingly self-possessed. She was indeed, as *Vanity Fair* reported, freakishly beautiful, extremely thin except for her chest, which was suspended over what looked like a 12-inch waist. Nielsen was friendly, but not forthcoming. It became apparent that she had only consented to the interview to plug her film, *Red Sonja*, not the more newsworthy romance. In the meantime, secretaries from nearby offices passed back and forth taking a peek at this new cynosure.

There was almost no way to research the actress's life, since she hadn't granted interviews before, and her modelling career had been confined to Scandinavia. Her prior life was a closed book. When I asked about previous romances, she refused comment. I thought it was out of loyalty to her possibly jealous new boyfriend. I'd later find out a more compelling and embarrassing reason.

The young and not so young lovers had met in the spring amid a romantic downpour of rain and raging hormones. Six months later, on 15 December 1985, they were married at the home of the groom's friend, *Rocky* producer Irwin Winkler. The marriage began with Stallone's best friend begging him to call off the wedding and ended 584 days later with Stallone publicly wishing he had heeded his friend's advice.

The actor's closest friend, Tony Munafo, began his association with Stallone two decades ago as bodyguard and since then has been promoted to associate producer of many of the actor's films. They remain best friends. The hulking Munafo, who has also had bit parts in his pal's movies, served as best man at the wedding. In the Rolls Royce ride to Winkler's home, Munafo went down on his knees and beseeched his buddy to leave the bride at the altar, actually a trelliswork overlooking the ocean.

'I begged him not to marry Gitte [Nielsen]. I knew she was going to be bad for him. I got bad vibes about her from the beginning. She hated me. I always treated Gitte very nice, but she knew I didn't trust her,' Munafo said. 'Don't do this!' Munafo pleaded. He gave up, realising, 'When you're in love, you're in love. Sly really loved that woman.'

Stallone *was* smitten. Before the relationship crashed, he described his infatuation with the gorgeous Amazon, and it wasn't just her beauty that bonded them. 'She's got it all,' he told *Rolling Stone* in 1985. 'She has heart, humour, beauty, athletic prowess, maternal instincts. She's very family oriented. And she's classically true to her man – I mean, really dedicated to the maintaining and prolonging of this relationship. There's a permanency about it. I have not gone out [?] or nothing. It's the same individual – and wonderfully – for ten months!'

The pair bonded even more strongly when he ended up in hospital after the injury to his heart while filming *Rocky IV*. Stallone credited his then girlfriend with literally saving his life. He had wanted to leave the hospital and return to the set immediately after the doctors told him he hadn't suffered a heart attack. Nielsen camped out in his hospital room and somehow forced him to remain there for a few more days to recuperate. Stallone's doctor later told him that if he hadn't followed Nielsen's advice and returned to the set sooner, he would have died.

Nielsen saved his life, but ultimately broke his heart. Eight months later, Stallone's laundry list of love for Nielsen would sound ironic as he and others aired their grievances about Nielsen's behaviour during the short-lived marriage.

Nielsen had refused to mention any previous boyfriends when I interviewed her, perhaps because she was still married at the time to the father of her son Julian in Denmark. Her vaunted maternal instincts didn't stop her from leaving pre-schooler Julian behind to pursue a career – and Stallone – in America. Her besotted new husband asserted that Danish law did not allow her to take the baby out of the country because her ex-husband had custody of the child. Nancy Collins, the savvy *Rolling Stone* reporter who quoted Stallone's claim, noted parenthetically that the Danish Consulate told her custody is awarded to the most fit parent, who is allowed to take the child abroad.

Almost before the wedding cake was stale, rumours of Nielsen's philanderings surfaced not just in the tabloids but in the legitimate press as well. The list of her alleged lovers suggested a woman of Renaissance, possibly gargantuan, tastes.

On her alleged 'to-do' (or already done) list were Eddie Murphy, her co-star in *Beverly Hills Cop II*; Tony Scott, the director of the film; and Kelly Sahnger, her secretary, whose breast augmentation surgery Nielsen had allegedly paid for.

Like a lioness guarding her cub, Jacqueline Stallone publicly castigated her daughter-in-law in any venue that would quote her. Jackie *is* very quotable. She told *Vanity Fair*, the Tiffany's of glossy celebrity magazines and as far from the tabloids as, well, Tiffany's is from paste jewellery, 'I warned [her son] about Brigitte. She came over here [to America] with not one honourable intention. There's not an honest bone in her body. But he thought she was this perfect woman . . . she humiliated him. She started cheating on him on their honeymoon. Back in Hollywood, she'd stay out all night dancing and go home with every jerk in town. She was even buying other guys gifts with his credit card.'

Another magazine quoted Jackie as having seen Nielsen and her secretary, Sahnger, in bed together. In a phone interview from Rome, where she was hosting a variety show, Nielsen flat out told me, 'I am not a lesbian! If I were a homosexual, these are not the times to hide it; I would say "yes" and "*basta*"!' Nielsen claimed Stallone's mother was 'insanely jealous' of their relationship. She also told me, but my editors at the magazine deleted the quote to avoid a lawsuit, that she suspected the senior Mrs Stallone was 'mentally ill'.

Eddie Murphy was horrified at the groundless rumours that he had romanced his beautiful co-star on the set of *Beverly Hills Cop II*. Stallone and Murphy had, in fact, been confidants. Both men suffered from clinical depression and had traded notes on their mutual affliction. When Murphy read in the press that he was supposedly stepping out with a good friend's wife, he called Stallone on the phone to deny the affair. He even went over to Stallone's home.

'He thought I fucked his wife,' Murphy recalled. 'He heard the rumour and believed it. He came after me and said, "*YOU FUCKED MY WIFE!*" I said, "Down, brother, I didn't fuck your wife!" We talked about it, but I guess somewhere in the back of his head, he'll never really know the truth. Sly and I liked each other too, but after the weirdness with Brigitte, it was ruined.

'I didn't fuck her. Did I ever want to fuck Gitte?' Murphy asked rhetorically. The answer was an unequivocal no. He was on record as not being attraced to white women, and his track record in the romance department backed him up. 'Gitte . . . is not my type. She was married. And married to somebody who was my friend. I'm not that kind of guy.'

The allegations frazzled Stallone so much that when Murphy showed up at several parties, Stallone left immediately.

The affair with Tony Scott was not so vehemently denied. One well-connected socialite told me, 'I can't imagine Brigitte would leave one of the most powerful actors in town unless she had a better offer from Scott. He's a hot director and makes much better movies than Stallone. I mean, how many girlfriends of a gun-crazed vigilante can she play?'

The socialite referred to their post-*Rocky IV* collaboration on *Cobra*, written by Stallone and directed by *Rambo*'s George Cosmatos. With that pedigree and on the heels of *Rocky IV* and *Rambo*'s box-office triumphs, *Cobra* seemed like a sure thing. Stallone played a Los Angeles cop whose disregard for civil rights as he tracks down a serial killer makes Clint Eastwood's Dirty Harry seem like a bleeding heart liberal. Nielsen played the cop's arm ornament without much to do but look gorgeous on screen. The expensive *Cobra* barely uncoiled at the box-office and returned a fangless $16 million. If, as some claimed, her pursuit of Stallone had more to do with pursuing her career than her heart, *Cobra*'s failure suggested that Scott, not Stallone, might indeed be a more worthy object of the chase.

A colleague of Scott's directed my attention to the publicity photos for *Beverly Hills Cop II*, which featured shots of the director and the leading lady together. 'Just look at the contact sheets . . . it's palpable – you can see Brigitte and Scott were falling in love.' Maybe they were. Maybe they weren't. If there was an affair, it didn't last long. Soon, Nielsen was dating again and eventually married a professional football player, Mark Gastineau, which at the very least spiked rumours that the Danish actress was a lesbian.

Despite the mudslinging from Stallone's camp, Nielsen cleaned up when she finally split with her husband. The divorce settlement awarded her $6 million – not bad work for 548 days of wedded bliss and bluster. The money, however, meant nothing to Stallone. He felt publicly humiliated and hinted in interviews that the break had traumatised him. The usually voluble interviewee spoke elliptically when he discussed the psychological damage the relationship had caused him.

At the beginning of the romance, Stallone said, 'Anyone who doesn't like Gitte is crazy.' By the end, he felt that *he* was the crazy one. Or as *Esquire* neatly put it, the marriage ended 'with him watching *Gaslight* and identifying with Ingrid Bergman'. The divorce became final in January 1988, but they had separated the previous summer.

No one, not even his outspoken mother, had apparently had the nerve to mention the rumours to the powerful star. He noticed smirks and sidelong glances that he later felt hid delight over his obtuseness. 'People took glee in it, revelled in the fact that I had been getting everything my way for so long.' And now, so-called friends revelled in the fact that he was getting something else this time – the shaft.

While friends and family publicly criticised his ex, Stallone remained the gentleman. He refused to badmouth Nielsen and only described his feelings about himself, not his feelings about her. 'I took a little fucking jog through *Dante's Inferno* and came out the other end,' he said, still hurting two years after the split.

Three years later, Stallone continued to speak in generalities about his ex-wife's behaviour. But time, rather than healing all wounds, seemed to have inflamed them. Even more bitterly than the year before, he performed this post-mortem on the relationship: 'My marriage to her rates with the riddle of the Sphinx. I fell madly in love with an ideal of physical perfection. It was devastating. What I thought was perfection turned into some rolling carnival of horrors put out on public display to be mocked. It had catastrophic effects on me in the area of bonding of the souls. I've lost the ability to be totally subservient to my heart.'

Maybe his heart became dysfunctional, but parts lower south continued to function magnificently. Regarding the break up, he said, 'If this had happened to anyone else, it would be called a tragedy. When it happens to me, it's entertainment.' That may be because after the split, Stallone provided so *much* 'entertainment' for himself and copy for the press with a succession of girlfriends who seemed to live on the cover of *Vogue*. Less than a year after the divorce's allegedly catastrophic effects on his ability to bond, he was bonding with so many women *People* magazine felt compelled to run 'The Official Sly Stallone 1988 Dating Calendar' with illustrations of his dates. There was one beauty per month, sometimes more. The magazine archly quoted him as saying at the beginning of the year, 'I will not date bimbos or gold-diggers any more,' then ran a three-page spread of his dates, without categorising them as either.

'Miss January & February' was Cornelia Guest, a wealthy socialite who dabbled in journalism and partied as her serious career. Gameshow hostess Vanna White held the 'Miss April' title. There were two title-holders for May, celebrity ex-wife Alana Hamilton Stewart (formerly Mrs George Hamilton and Mrs Rod Stewart) and actress-model Devin Devasquez. The only date that year who didn't seem to have aspirations in front of the camera had the gloriously *double-entendre* name of Suzanne LaCock, a television producer.

The most important calendar entry, however, was 'Miss September', model Jennifer Flavin. Despite the competition, Miss September would prevail and win the all-around title of Mrs Sylvester Stallone. All it took was nine years of public and private humiliation.

# Chapter Fourteen

# Rambo Tries Arm Wrestling

As Stallone's personal life revolved on a merry-go-round of casual dates and fear of intimacy, his professional life also suffered from lack of purpose and direction. While his romantic entanglements lacked depth and endurance, his film choices suggested he was similarly just 'going through the motions' when he appeared on screen. When he revisited the boxing ring or Rambo's turf, his movies did well. In any other venue, the public ignored him and the critics derided him. When he stretched in an atypical role, he was criticised for overreaching and overestimating his talents. When he played it safe and armed himself with boxing gloves or Uzis, fans cheered. The press yelled, 'Sell out!'

His public humiliation by Nielsen in 1987 continued with a professional humiliation called *Over the Top*, an expensive blue-collar epic about arm wrestling. Stallone played a truck driver who tries to win his son's respect by winning an arm wrestling contest. The most noteworthy thing about the project seemed to be the star's fee, a then record-breaking $12 million.

Menahem Golan, the colourful chairman of Cannon Films and the owner of a chain of movie theatres in Israel, came to America with a huge chequebook and aspirations of becoming a major player. He was also starstruck. His $12 million offer to Stallone was resented by the studios because it upped every other star's asking price. Golan's decision to direct the film seemed even loonier. At the time Golan had feelers – and big money offers – out to other superstars, who failed to fall under his financial spell. When I interviewed him in his offices near Hollywood in 1984 for UPI, he told me Jack Nicholson had 'expressed interest' in a film based on the Saul Bellow classic, *Henderson the Rain King*. I checked with Nicholson's manager at the time, Sandy Bresler, to confirm the story. Bresler told me that Golan had a habit of making such claims and Bresler had told him to stop talking about associations that did not exist.

Stallone co-wrote *Over the Top* with a masterful screenwriter, Stirling Silliphant, who had both prestigious credits like *In the Heat of the Night* and great commercial success with popcorn hits like *The Poseidon Adventure* and *The Towering Inferno*. *Over the Top*, however, bottomed out at the box-office with only $16 million, barely enough to cover the star's fee. In a blistering review, *Newsweek* suggested that if the star really wanted to stretch, his next project should focus on championship horseshoe-pitching. Director Golan eventually left Hollywood and returned to his native Israel, where his real expertise, operating movie theatres, found a happier home.

A year later, Stallone fled to safer terrain, but he didn't find much security with Rambo's third trip to beat up bad guys in the Third World. *Rambo III* became one of the most expensive films of its day, with a $60 million budget. The script became notorious for giving the title character only 163 lines. *Time* magazine estimated that Stallone was paid half a million dollars per sentence! The story of Rambo fighting Russian commies again – this time in in Afghanistan – seemed sadly out of touch. The first *Rambo* tapped into a renewal of patriotism and conservatism during the early Reagan years. By 1988, the Soviet Union had already begun to withdraw from its version of Vietnam, Afghanistan. *Rambo III*'s boogieman was almost gone by the time the movie hit theatres since Gorbachev's *glasnost* had already defanged the Red Menace Rambo loved to fight.

Moviegoers had no interest in a tiny Third World country in diminishing peril, but *Rambo III* did get a lot of attention due to troubled reports from the set. Only two weeks into filming, Stallone fired the director, Russell Mulcahy, and most of the crew. The official reason had nothing to do with the star or the usual 'artistic differences'. The director was several days behind schedule and that's why he was replaced by second unit director Peter MacDonald, according to the official line. The unofficial story claimed Stallone loathed the dailies.

*People* magazine at the time described a superstar who was reaching Elvis-like isolation. His entourage included ten bodyguards. Psychologists who are experts on obsessive-compulsive behaviour might explain another quirk reported in the press at this time. The star took five showers a day.

Unlike an arm wrestling movie, a new *Rambo* must have seemed like a sure bet when the studio wagered $60 million on the vigilante's continuing popularity. It bet wrong. The public made a touchy-feely film like *Rainman* the number one box-office and Oscar champ of the year with a domestic gross of more than $200 million. The muscular vigilante only scored $54 million in the US, not enough to cover the budget.

Stallone decided to disarm himself for his next film. If the public liked an underdog loaded with high tech weapons fighting against all odds, maybe they would like the star battling even worse odds, this time in prison. And with a personality. Unlike Rambo, Stallone had a lot more to say in his next film, 1989's *Lock Up*. He played a lovable con with only six months left of his sentence. He has a loving gilfriend (Darlanne Fluegel) waiting on the outside. The warden (Donald Sutherland) has a long-standing grudge against the model prisoner, Stallone. A prison break provides the excuse for Sutherland to extend Stallone's stay in jail.

The *New York Times* praised Stallone's convict for showing some of Rocky Balboa's old charm, but dismissed the film for making as much plot sense as the *Rambo* films, where bullets always miss the hero. Despite the *Rocky* flavour, *Lock Up* failed to attract Rocky's fans, with a final US take of $23 million.

At this point, Stallone's nervous handlers huddled and decided the star needed to stretch a lot more. They decided to rearm the hero, but go upscale with dialogue and wardrobe.

The gimmick for 1989's *Tango & Cash* shows that Stallone's willingness to stretch was incremental rather than dramatically elastic. After one too many trips to the jungle and the ring, the *New York Times* in 1989 declared Stallone 'a man in desperate need of career advice'. His advisors told him to play a Los Angeles narcotics detective who wears Armani suits and designer glasses. And instead of having to carry the picture (and weaponry) all by himself, he was paired with Kurt Russell, a fellow narco cop who played a slob Oscar Madison to the new Felix Ungar, Stallone.

Stallone's Armani togs don't stay on for long in *Tango & Cash*. The star had spent too many hours in the gym to hide under three-piece suits, even if another famous Italian had designed them. Soon, Russell and Stallone end up in prison, where they get to strip down to form-fitting tanktops and even take a shower together. The public ignored the critics, or maybe the reviews mentioning all that male nudity brought in female heavy-breathers. For whatever demographic reasons, *Tango & Cash* accumulated a tidy $63 million in the US and $40 million abroad.

Ticket sales didn't give the star the courage to stretch a bit more. The end of the Cold War at the beginning of the new decade meant Rambo had become a relic. So Stallone went back to his other popular incarnation. He returned to the ring.

In 1990, *Rocky V* reflected an unreflective artist who had degenerated into self-parody. A sight-gag way back in 1983's *Airplane II* showed a movie poster of an emaciated senior citizen wearing boxing gloves and trunks. The film's title: *Rocky XXXVIII*. The gag came a bit closer to reality with *Rocky V*.

The star, of course, wasn't emaciated, but the storyline was. Stallone was too long in the tooth by now to be believable as a heavyweight contender. The film begins with Rocky broke and homeless. He moves back to the slums of Philadelphia and decides to train a heavyweight with promise, Tommy Gunn (John Wayne's nephew, Tommy Morrison). The ensuing morality play has Gunn betraying Rocky after being wooed by a more successful boxing promoter patterned after Don King. The most interesting thing about the project involved the casting of Stallone's son Sage, who had appeared in *Rocky III*. If Sage's performance in *Rocky V* seemed particularly heart-felt, it may have been because it was also autobiographical.

In the fifth film of the ring cycle, Sage's Rocky Jr screams at Rocky *père*, 'You never spent time with me! You never spent time with my mother!' Sage should have demanded credit as co-writer. The youngster later told interviewers he was describing his real-life relationship with his father when he made his on-screen accusations. 'He was never around when I was growing up. He was always off making movies. I used to hang out with the help in the house,' Sage said.

Stallone did take time to give his son advice on the set. Accompanied by a bodyguard, Sage visited his father's trailer, where dad told him, 'Remember, DTA' Sage didn't remember the acronym, so his father spelled it out. 'Don't trust anyone.' Sage left, and Stallone explained to a visiting journalist, 'Sage is the benefactor [sic] of all my mistakes. Everyone thinks he'll be Son of Rocky in the next sequel, and probably he thinks so, too.' Stallone made it clear the youngster wouldn't appear in *Rocky VI*, if there ever was one. Being typecast as Rocky Jr, Stallone said, 'would have a Vesuvian effect on him. He'd be buried in my hypercritical lava.'

Although he never bothered to move the family out of what he considered the corrupting influence of the film capital and the family's affluence, the father still worried about his son's distorted view of the world. Stallone said, 'Growing up in Hollywood, the first word you learn isn't "mommy". It's "limo".'

While Stallone worried about Sage being typecast as little Rocky, he didn't have any qualms about nepotism in general. Six years later he would hire his heir again for *Daylight*.

Despite the interesting autobiographical subtext, the actual text of *Rocky V* was a downer. Stallone said, 'I was naïve to believe there's an audience who wanted to watch a man crash and burn whom they've come to know for 14 years. I think there's a resistance to people seeing the older Elvis or the dour Charlie Chaplin. I don't think they really want to see the dark side of their heroes.'

They certainly didn't. Rocky's fifth trip to the ring drew the smallest crowd of the series, with US ticket sales of only $41 million.

More than a little stretching was called for. With his next two films, Stallone would bend over backwards to get the audience's attention. Would they notice his gymnastics enough to show up and take a peek at their idol's new incarnation?

# Chapter Fifteen

# Stallion in Drawing-Room = Bull in China Shop

It's difficult to figure out Stallone's decision to try light comedy at the beginning of this decade. Twice. The public had rejected his previous essay at farce, *Rhinestone*, eight years earlier.

Maybe 1991's *Oscar* would grant him a second chance. It was a comedy based on a classic 1958 French farce of the same name, which was turned into a film nine years later. Stallone feigning farce wasn't quite as loony as it sounded, since in *Oscar* he would be playing a character closer to home thematically than a Parisian bedroom. Stallone stars as gangster Angelo 'Snaps' Provolone, who is trying to fulfil a deathbed promise to his father to go legit. A country and western singing cabdriver sounded like a high concept from hell. A gangster doing Noel Coward or Feydeau probably gave Disney executives a hellish case of the hives, but at least the star didn't sing in this one.

Stallone knew he had to do something to redirect his career. His prescription called for reinventing himself on screen. 'With *Rocky* and *Rambo*, I'd fallen into a sense of self-parody. When I say "reinvent", I mean I'm gonna scrape away the image. To me, an actor is like a sculpture of a man with a chisel, moulding himself in the likeness he wants to be in. That's what acting can sometimes do to you – you mould yourself into a certain image, and if it has been successful, you don't want to stray too far from it. You sort of become cast in stone. Now I have to shatter the mould, go back to what I think I can do best – and that is a sense of improvisational acting. That's when I let loose, become unselfconscious.'

His choice of director for *Oscar* raised eyebrows. John Landis had proved himself a master of farce with *Animal House*, but that had been 13 years earlier, and Landis's speciality involved toilet humour, not witty repartee. During filming, Stallone began to worry if the vehicle and the driver he had chosen were a mistake. 'With . . . *Oscar*, director John Landis pushed me until I thought, "My God, the acting police are gonna come and take us away. You know, we're really overacting here."'

*Oscar* was a comedy of errors and a bedroom farce. Set in New York in the 1930s, the convoluted plot revolved around the gangster's attempt to gain respectability and marry off his daughter to an aristocrat. The daughter loves a downscale accountant who has stolen Stallone's money, etc, and the ensuing complications involved the classic slamming of bedroom doors and mistaken identities.

Stallone claimed he had more lines of dialogue than all his other films combined. 'It's comedy on diet pills. It's so fast, it's so furious and so absolutely confusing, it's almost like a magician's sleight of hand.' The actor hinted he was out of his depth and engaged in a bit of self-mocking much funnier than anything in *Oscar*. 'I tried to write in a crucifixion scene,' he said, referring to his Christ-like dip in a compost heap during *Rambo*, 'but they wouldn't let me.' The critics wrote the crucifixion scenes instead: *Variety* called it 'hollow at the core . . . Stallone . . . does no more than a serviceable job in getting across the humour.' The *Los Angeles Times* damned him with faint praise: 'Stallone is actually borderline acceptable as a farce hero . . . which is not really saying much. [After *Rhinestone*, moviegoers] know how low expectations can legitimately be when Sly gets in a chuckling mood.' The audience rejected this Chatty Cathy in a zoot suit, and ticket sales of $20 million reflected that.

So, moviegoers don't like their beefcake as the butt of jokes. What's a floundering superstar to do? Try another comedy, even more farcical? At the point, an industry analyst wondered if

Stallone had one of the Three Stooges on the payroll as scriptreader and manager. His next film, *Stop! Or My Mom Will Shoot*, in 1992, wasn't quite the departure *Oscar*'s salute to comedy had been. This time the yuks would be punctuated with bullets.

The audience was still not amused.

The high concept involved a buddy cop movie with a twist. The buddy was the cop's mother. Stallone is a daredevil cop for the LAPD. His mom, Tutti Bomowski, comes to visit from Newark, New Jersey, and ends up riding shotgun in her son's cop car after she witnesses a driveby shooting. Tutti was played by Estelle Getty, famous in the US as the senile Sophia on the hit sitcom, *The Golden Girls*. Since Stallone's audience by now was firmly located overseas, the idea of a casting a senior citizen well known only in the US seemed questionable.

The critics and industry observers suspected Stallone was trying to tap into the same audience as another muscled star, Arnold Schwarzenegger, with his excursions into light comedy, *Twins* and *Kindergarten Cop*. In fact, two of the four writers credited on *Stop!* also worked on *Twins*.

The *New York Times*'s Vincent Canby stated the consensus and the obvious about *Stop! Or My Mom Will Shoot*, calling it 'terrible' and 'bottom drawer'. The *Los Angeles Times* decried the writers giving filthy dialogue – especially about bodily functions – to America's favourite Golden Girl. The public didn't accept Stallone doing Schwarzenegger Lite and the expensive comedy grossed only $28 million in the US. The actor didn't disagree with the public or critical reaction. Years later, he confessed it was his worst film. 'Without a doubt. Even in some of the films that have not worked, there's maybe 20 minutes that I appreciate just for the audacity. Even in *Rhinestone* – the gall to put on that cowboy outfit. I thought, "Well, that was a ballsy move." But with *Stop! Or My Mom Will Shoot*, I thought, "How did this happen?"'

By 1992, Stallone was in trouble. When he stretched with a new screen character, the audience contracted. Witty or grim, farcical or ferocious, moviegoers didn't want Rocky, Rambo or a buffed Noel Coward.

Stallone took full blame for his meandering career. 'I've made some mistakes. There've been some disappointments. Every mistake I could have made, I made,' he said in 1992 looking back on the Reagan era's Decade of Greed as his Decade of Arrogance. 'I *was* arrogant. I was petty. I was selfish. I was into perks and being flattered. I was insulated and I didn't listen or I listened to the wrong people.'

Hollywood's power brokers agreed and called him down for the count – but of course, not for attribution. You never know when today's has-been will be tomorrow's comeback kid with *Pulp Fiction* (John Travolta) or *The Nutty Professor* (Eddie Murphy). An unnamed Hollywood agent told the *New York Times*, 'He's the new Burt Reynolds . . . I think he's a diminishing asset. With every film he does, he goes down a little further.'

Stallone decided to go up a lot – literally – in his next film, *Cliffhanger*, in 1993. And if the audience refused to let him challenge himself dramatically with comedy, he would challenge himself physically. But this time, instead of transforming his body at the gym, he decided to tackle a phobia the public hitherto had been unaware of, a fear of heights. Roughly 50 per cent of the 'cliffhanging' in *Cliffhanger* was done by Stallone, not his stunt double.

As its title suggests, Stallone would spend a lot of time hanging off the edge of an Alp to film the movie about a US Forest Ranger in the Colorado Rockies (Europe's mountain range was cheaper to shoot on than America's Continental Divide). Stallone's Gabe Walker, a National Park Service rescue ranger, battles narco-terrorists looking for drug money accidentally dumped out of a plane over the Rockies.

*Cliffhanger* was an even bigger risk for Carolco, the production company that produced the *Rambo* series. The company was in the middle of its umpteenth financial crisis, and *Cliffhanger*'s $60 million budget represented a huge gamble. For insurance, Carolco hired the superhot director of *Die Hard II*, Renny Harlin. So many of Stallone's previous flops had been directed either by first-time directors who could be managed by the star, or veterans whose own resumés were in so much trouble, they wouldn't give the star a fight over artistic control. Neither a novice nor a desperate veteran would dare to engage in shoving matches with the actor as had happened during his rising star days.

Carolco's gamble paid off. *Cliffhanger* grossed $84 million in the US alone and typically did better in Europe, where American action stars are even more popular. (That's why Jean-Claude Van Damme and Steven Seagal continue to work. Their martial arts and mayhem movies bomb in America, but flourish overseas.) *Cliffhanger*'s foreign tally reached a dizzying $171 million. Director Renny Harlin said, 'Sly wanted the big comeback. He wanted to say to the audience, "OK, here's the Stallone you learned to love in Rocky."'

Reports of the actor's career death had been greatly exaggerated, but he was surprised just how low his stock had fallen before this Alpine Rockie turned him into a one-man bull market. 'When *Cliffhanger* came out, the people who write the articles started venting what they had really been thinking about me. It was like "Stallone back from the grave, after a totally dismal five years!" I'm reading this and I'm like, "God! If I'd known it was like that, I would have killed myself!" Jesus! It woulda been a situation like, "Take all sharp objects out of the room." I woulda plunged a dagger in my heart!'

Stallone didn't learn the complete lesson from the success of *Cliffhanger*. Sharp objects may have been snatched out of his presence when his next film came out.

*Cliffhanger* demonstrated that the audience wanted their action hero back, but it was important to have him supervised by an accomplished director with the courage and clout to just say no. *Demolition Man*, which followed *Cliffhanger* the same year, was another action movie, but with two big differences, one lethal, the other high concept. The high concept cast Stallone as a police detective (surprise!) wrongly convicted of murder, sentenced to be frozen alive, then thawed out in the twenty-first century to track down a terrorist (Wesley Snipes), also recently defrosted. Adding sci-fi to the action genre would be a synergistic mix, Stallone and his advisors presumed. And it came with the services of the A-list producer of big budget B-movies, Joel Silver (*Die Hards*).

Unfortunately, Stallone and Silver chose first-time movie director, Marco Brambilla. *Demolition Man* earned *Cobra* and *Lock Up*-style reviews – poisonous. *Demolition Man*'s US gross of $58 million didn't even cover the $60 million budget. Its overseas haul salvaged enough of the star's self-confidence to keep him in the action genre for his next film, but this time no expensive high concepts like defrosting the star would be involved.

*The Specialist* (1994) was set firmly in the present, in Miami's affluent subculture of the cocaine cartel. Instead of sci-fi, this film's gimmick involved casting an A-list actress, Sharon Stone, instead of the usual disposable starlet, who invariably fell into the 'Whatever Happened to . . .' coffee-table books.

In *The Specialist*, Sharon Stone, still hot from 1992's biggest hit, *Basic Instinct*, hires Stallone, a demolitions expert, to, well, blow up the Colombian drugrunners who murdered her parents while she watched as a child. The plot was wafer thin, but the sex scenes between the superstars got a lot of attention, especially one long sequence where they shower together. Panning the film, the *New York Times* derided this contest between bathroom bodybuilders. ' . . . Towards the end there is a nude shower scene, revealing that Ray and May [Stallone and Stone] must spend a fortune on personal trainers. The camera makes sure to get a good shot of Ray's bare buttocks.' The *Times*'s female reviewer, Caryn James, failed to mention that as the ranking star in the bathroom, Stallone got to show more flesh than his leading lady.

Maybe that's why preview audiences voted for less time in the shower. Stallone said he wanted 'something semi-erotic [but] not a full-on screw film'. The preview cards said turn off the faucet. Or as the star paraphrased the verdict: 'We don't want to see John Wayne fornicating, or Sylvester Stallone. It's the *Rocky* curse and blessing.'

The critic for the *New York Times* tried to teach Stallone a lesson he should have learned from *Cliffhanger* and failed to apply to *The Specialist* and his follow-up film, *Judge Dredd*. 'Everything in Mr Stallone's career suggests he needs a strong director, like Renny Harlin, who surrounded him with superbly paced action and evoked a witty performance in *Cliffhanger*. [*The Specialist*'s director] Luis Llosa doesn't come close here.'

Even with less screen time, Stone's presence guaranteed *The Specialist* a monster opening, first place, with $14 million during its first three days in release and a worldwide total of $113 million.

Stallone went back to the future with *Judge Dredd*, a twenty-second century vigilante who applied a Charles Bronson sense of justice to crime. The title character was not only jurist, he was also arresting officer, jury and executioner economically rolled into one. The film represented a costly gamble, with another make-or-break budget of $65 million, and an iffy high concept. *Judge Dredd* was based on a comic book character, but the super anti-hero was only popular in the UK. The judge was barely known in the US, and the American public didn't seem to want to know his film incarnation. *Judge Dredd*, the film, grossed an embarrassing $34 million in the US, but a face-saving $80 million overseas.

*Daily Variety* not only slammed the film, but questioned the marketing sanity of its distributor, Disney. Calling the film a 'thunderous, unoriginal futuristic hardware show for teenage boys', the trade paper wondered why the studio's censors had left in so much violence and profanity that the teen-targeted pic received an R-rating. The rating meant anyone under 18 years of age had to suffer the ultimate embarrassment, bringing mom or dad along to the theatre.

\* \* \*

Stallone thought he was making an artistic departure with his next film, *Assassins*, describing it as an '*existentialist* action film with a philosophy of "What I am not, I *will* be some day."' Stallone plays a contract killer, at the top of his profession, who is challenged by an ambitious, younger hit man.

The actor called the formulaic plot 'Hitchockian'. At least this time he had the directing services of Richard Donner, who brought clout and a track record to the set with credits like *Superman* and *Lethal Weapon*. And to broaden the audience net,

Antonio Banderas, another Latin stud with a younger demographic, was cast as the junior assassin in an attempt to generate the same heat with European audiences that Stone's participation had in *The Specialist*. Unfortunately, an 18 certificate shower scene with these two stars wouldn't create the same kind of synergy as Stallone and Stone sudsing each other up in the bathroom.

*Assassins* reminded the ageing superstar of his mortality. Although he and Banderas enjoyed a friendly collaboration, the rivalry existed, perhaps more in the older man's mind than in Banderas's. A crew member said, 'Sly thinks Antonio's great – I mean, who doesn't like Antonio? – but, like the relationship of the two guys in the movie, this time Sly's really working on his chops because Antonio's a young, gorgeous actor who could run off with the movie.'

An Olympic sprinter couldn't have performed that feat. *Assassins* performed worse than its immediate predecessor, *Judge Dredd*, with only $28 million in the US. Banderas's participation did help the film's performance abroad for a respectable world-wide tally of $76 million.

In 1996, Stallone tried a subgenre of the action film, the disaster movie. *Daylight* had the hero battling a flooded tunnel linking New York and New Jersey. Disasters cost a lot to film, and *Daylight* weighed in at a budget-busting $93 million. It earned only $33 million in the US and $119 million overseas, which made the project an iffy, break-even proposition for its backers.

Stallone felt buried under the special effects and the unoriginal storyline of *Daylight*. In one of many public *mea culpas*, he later said about the shoot, 'Probably the single toughest film I've ever done. I now understand how Poe felt every day. This was a premature burial.'

Pundits were applying the same metaphor to his career. With one unchallenging role after another and with dwindling ticket sales, Stallone was desperate to reinvent himself. But this time it would take more than hot sex in a private bathroom or a flood in public transit.

In early 1997, with *Daylight* long gone from theatres, an

anonymous producer lumped Stallone in the same gilt-gone-to-rust company of another unlikely superstar, Arnold Schwarzenegger. 'Look, Sly, is a great guy. He was written off when he did those stupid comedies. But then he came back with *Cliffhanger* and that shut everybody up. But the problem is he's 50. Unlike Travolta [then 42], a comeback at his age is really tough.

'The big question for all these guys like Sly and Arnold is, where do you go when you've sold yourself to the public one way for so long?'

Where *do* you go? Stallone decided to go straight to the fridge to rehabilitate an imperfect career – and trash his perfect body.

# Chapter Sixteen

# Method Eating

Industry pros seemed delighted to comment on Stallone's professional demise – always under cover of anonymity, of course. A senior executive at Paramount in 1997 didn't mince words, although he also insisted on not being identified. The executive's terse post-mortem on the body of Stallone's work: 'Face it, it's over. Next.'

In early 1997, Stallone wasn't ready to retire or give interviews for his obituary, but the profoundly dispirited artist said that his typecasting as a no-talk-all-action stereotype had been an 'empty experience', and despite the financial rewards from playing variations on his greatest hits, his movie grosses amounted to 'fool's gold'.

Stallone's then agent, Arnold Rifkin, spoke up and on the record, promising that his client's obituary writers were premature. 'Wait until his fans see him in *Cop Land*. Sly wants a chance to try new things, a change. Just give him a chance to be what he wants to be,' Rifkin almost pleaded with a reporter from the *Los Angeles Times*.

What the fans saw in *Cop Land* shocked them. What Stallone saw when he looked at himself in the mirror on the set of the film didn't shock him. It sent him into paroxysms of self-loathing. When the actor showed up on the set of *Daylight* in 1996, he boasted a 30-inch waist. Only a year later, for *Cop Land*, he had gained 40 pounds and saw his midsection balloon to a Falstaffian 39 inches.

Just as beefing up his body seemed to help *Rocky* and *Rambo* sequels beef up the box-office, Stallone hoped to salvage a drifting career with another dramatic physical transformation. But this time, lard, not lean cuisine, would help flesh out his character, Freddy Heflin, the timid, partially deaf police chief of a small New Jersey town. Where Rambo and Rocky were all action, Stallone's fat cop was mostly inaction. The New Jersey suburb he presides over doesn't really need a chief of police. The locals are armed and know how to use their weapons. The town is a bedroom community for tough New York City cops who have fled the Rotten Apple's mean streets for tranquil suburbia in nearby New Jersey. Because of his hearing impairment, Freddy long ago had failed the physical for his dream job on a big city police force. Now, he worships the cops who work across the river but live in his town. Freddy's job seems to consist of letting these off-duty cops off the hook when they get pulled over for speeding or crashing a red light in his jurisdiction. That is, until the dim bulb Heflin gradually discovers the big city cops he idolises are engaged in big time corruption. By film's end, the stolid, passive police chief turns into a suburban Rambo.

To get *out* of shape for the role of Freddy, Stallone abandoned his home away from home – the gym – and set up shop at the Canadian Pancake House on Second Avenue in New York City. Before hitting the set in nearby New Jersey, Stallone would scoff down a breakfast of five pancakes smothered with peanut butter and whipped cream, a bowl of oatmeal, two bagels with more peanut butter, ten fried eggs, french fries and cheesecake! This binge diet horrified the Stallone of the egg-yolk-gulping days in the *Rocky* era. The actor's weight jumped from 173 to 200 pounds-plus for *Cop Land*.

Stallone wanted the role so badly, he dropped his usual fee of $20 million and worked for union scale, about $50,000. 'It didn't even pay my secretary's salary,' he joked. The actor even agreed to audition for newcomer writer-director James

Mangold, who had only one previous art house film to his credit.

Mangold had the temerity and self-possession to order the superstar to lose the muscle and find the fat. 'Sly when he's lean has such a heroic visage, and I didn't want that,' Mangold, 34, said. 'I wanted to shoot a close-up of his face and feel Lays potato chips, feel McDonald's. I wanted to feel a normal American face.' Mangold turned out to be as demanding as any personal trainer, but instead of dragging his client to the gym, he phoned for a daily report on the actor's calorie intake.

Stallone said Mangold 'would call up on the phone: "Have you gained weight?" I said, "I'm up to 185 . . . 191. Good enough?"

"No," Mangold said. "You've got to gain a little more." I said, "Please, I can't."' The director came for a visit to see for himself if Stallone had 'grown' into his new role. The actor ended up standing in profile and sticking out his paunch. The director wanted more. Mangold said, 'Well, it's kind of impressive, but . . .'

In theory, Stallone agreed with the director. The external image would reflect the inner man. He just didn't realise how much it would affect his self-esteem. 'I knew I had to do something that was physically just so different that it would affect the acting. If you put on 30 pounds, you're going to talk differently, you're going to walk differently, you're going to think differently about yourself . . . You've got to mess up your body mechanics if you're going to do something different.'

He also messed up his mind in the process. It had been so many years since he had been a scrawny youth put down by parent and peers, Stallone forgot what having a negative body image felt like. As the scale neared 210 pounds, he began to remember.

The actor compared weight-training to drug-taking, and when he quit, he went through a withdrawal that was both psychological and physical. '[The gym] becomes as addicting as any kind of drug. Narcissism is as lethal a phenomenon as you can imagine. It taps into one's psyche and insecurities. As your body or the drugs wear off and you cannot maintain that superstar status, you begin to lose all self-esteem, all sense of presence.'

In a heart-to-heart interview with Susan Faludi, the author of several books on *women* and body image, Stallone confessed how much emotional armour his muscles had provided. When they were gone, he felt defenceless against feelings of physical and intellectual inadequacy which came roaring back from childhood. 'I thought the only way to override that was through creating an imposing exterior . . . And then taking this part, I didn't realise how extremely difficult it would be to change my shape and let it go. Then I realised I had been using it as a psychological tool for a very long time.'

Fabulously rich, engaged to a gorgeous model, Stallone still felt like a piece of (overweight) meat. It didn't help that when he arrived on the set, an unsympathetic crew member would shout, 'Fat man walking!' The earlier Stallone would have had the low-level employee fired. The new, serious actor used the taunts to keep himself – or at least the fat police chief he was playing – humble. 'There was absolutely no respect whatsoever,' Stallone said about the ridicule his new incarnation encountered. 'When I came in, there were all these sidelong glances and even though people knew I was in the movie, it didn't matter. It was, "Hey, you're not so special." Which was great, exactly what I was hoping would happen.'

Ray Liotta, who plays one of the New York City cops living in Stallone's town, said the star would buttonhole strangers and try to explain that this wasn't really him, just a character he was playing. Except of course, they were one and the same. Liotta recalled, 'He'd say, "Hey, I'm doing a movie, that's why I'm heavy." He'd say this to a perfect stranger.'

When Stallone was introduced to his leading lady, Anabella Sciorra, the first words out of his mouth were, 'Hi, I'm not usually this fat.' Sciorra thought to herself, 'Like I didn't know that already . . . But I guess he just wanted to make sure.'

Stallone was so embarrassed by his grotesque body image he only half-jokingly suggested, 'I should have gotten a little sign saying, "This isn't me. I'm doing this for a film."'

Eventually, this sort of reversible self-disfigurement became a healing rather than a hurting experience. 'I had to lose my pride and my self-image to play this part and when it was done, I felt better than I ever had before in my life. I no longer had to impress anyone. I could walk into a room and not make waves. It was a relief.' It also helped that his fiancée, Jennifer Flavin, was pregnant at the same time, and even the competitive Stallone couldn't compete with her stunning growth. Around Flavin, a once super-thin model, he still felt svelte. Maybe she was just being kind, but Flavin told him she found his fleshy body sexier than its lean incarnation. Unfortunately, she didn't let him know this until he had lost all the fat after the production wrapped. 'Why didn't you tell me before?', he asked, not that her preference would have kept him from the gym and restored physical perfection.

Stallone got so wrapped up in his personal transformation that just as he had once overdeveloped his body to the point of obsession and self-injury, he attacked gaining weight as though he were training for a fight – in this case, a true *heavy*weight bout. Finally, even the pushy director told him to put those doughnuts down.

In one scene, Stallone rolls over in bed with his pyjamas unbuttoned. His enormous gut tumbles out. A preview audience gasped. The scene had to be cut because it was so distracting. 'Sly's gut fell out of his T-shirt,' Mangold recalled, 'and we all went, "Wow! That's gonna be an amazing moment." But it became a moment that wasn't about the movie, it was about a superstar gaining weight. For an audience, that moment was . . . Stallone . . . with a gut!'

Physical inadequacy wasn't the only problem he had with self-esteem on the set. His co-stars included the most respected actor of his generation. Robert De Niro played an internal affairs detective investigating the dirty cops who live in Stallone's town. Harvey Keitel was a smarmy, corrupt cop who sweet-talks Stallone into looking the other way when he discovers that his big city heroes are venal villains.

'I never thought I'd get the chance to star with De Niro,' Stallone said, sounding like an aspiring – rather than mega – star whose box-office dwarfs De Niro's ten-fold.

Sharing the screen with De Niro, he added, was more terrifying than hanging from an alp in *Cliffhanger*. And this from a man who was phobic about heights. He was apparently even more phobic about superior talents. 'In *Cliffhanger*, I put my life in danger at least a dozen times, but in my estimation that didn't hold a hill of beans to a Robert De Niro acting moment.

'I must admit this – I've always been very envious of Harvey Keitel and De Niro . . . people that have really made a career doing things that are passionate and respected, and I thought, "I've got to try it one last time."'

His big dramatic scene with De Niro was filmed the second day of production. Adding to his nervousness was an A-list audience of studio executives who came to see one of the most respected artists in the business go *mano a mano* with one of the least respected. It could have been a scene from *Rocky*, but instead of his fists this time the underdog would have to rely on his acting. 'It seemed like every executive in Hollywood showed up on the set that day. I had rehearsed the scene in my head over and over again. It was almost like a heavyweight fight, with all the anticipation and the hype.

'I was intimidated. I was very self-conscious because I knew I was not going to be taken seriously. I would have to prove myself, and so there was fear and intimidation which I guess in the end helped because it made me work a little harder . . . it was the first time in my life I was surrounded by superior dramatic actors *period*,' Stallone confessed.

De Niro went out of his way to be unintimidating. A decade earlier, the Oscar-winner had been stand-offish when he first met Stallone. A mutual friend, director Brian De Palma, explained that De Niro wasn't aloof. 'It just takes six to seven years to get to know him,' De Palma told Stallone.

A decade later, De Niro still wasn't Mr Motor Mouth, but after working with him, Stallone figured out why. 'He saves all his normal conversational strength and things like that and puts it on the screen.' Despite his taciturn nature, after each shot, De Niro would let Stallone know if he had done a good job with an almost invisible gesture of praise or criticism. 'He would give me feedback at the end of each take with a certain gesture I don't even know if he was aware of.' De Niro, he added, was 'very, very, very, very kind'.

But not uncritical. Besides gestures, Stallone learned to read disapproval in his co-star's eyes. 'If Bobby didn't like a scene, it would be pretty apparent. There's a certain glassiness that comes over people's eyes. You know they can't wait for the scene to end so they can do another take.'

When the production wrapped, Stallone was in for another shock. As hard as it had been to add 40 pounds, it was torture to take it off. 'I thought it would be easy. It's hard; I've suffered.' After bingeing on pancakes and peanut butter, he forced himself to eat only one meal a day. He lived on the treadmill. 'Chasing the carrot,' as he put it. It took almost six months to lose the fat, which he estimated disappeared at the glacial speed of two pounds a week.

Dieting horrors paled compared to the press reaction. Harvey Weinstein, co-chairman of Miramax, which produced *Cop Land*, predicted that the character-driven film would put Stallone back on top just as *Pulp Fiction* had resuscitated John Travolta's career and burnished Bruce Willis's. Stallone hoped Weinstein was right. 'On the twentieth anniversary of *Rocky*, just maybe I'm going to be taken seriously again,' he said. (Actually, it was the twenty-first anniversary, but who's going to argue with a guy who can crack walnuts with his cleavage?)

Unfortunately, the critics didn't share Chairman Weinstein's bullishness or his star's hopefulness. Critics had reviled Stallone as an action star. They lampooned him as an 'inaction' star in *Cop Land*. The *Wall Street Journal* said, 'Sylvester Stallone . . . wanted to break out of the action mould . . . But for much of this tedious melodrama, you wonder if he'll break out of the *inaction* mould.' The *Los Angeles Times* said his performance was 'involving in individual moments, but not compelling as a whole . . . it ends up promising more than it can deliver.' The *Village Voice* stooped to *ad hominem* attacks and offered *Cop Land*'s writer-director a tip that came too late: 'A more skilled director than Mangold might have found a tactful way to tell Stallone that it's redundant for him to expend so much energy acting like a doofus since he already *is* a doofus.'

Not everyone panned Stallone's attempts to stretch somewhere else besides the gym. *Daily Variety* praised the film's 'stellar cast *led* by Sylvester Stallone . . . !' Considering that De Niro and Keitel were following, this was high praise indeed. London's usually cheeky *Time Out* magazine also felt the actor more than held his own against the real heavyweights in the film: '*Cop Land* works because as Keitel and company give explosive performances, Stallone's quiet, unflashy turn gives the film the anchor it needs.'

Since the star-heavy cast worked for scale, *Cop Land* cost only $28 million, despite expensive outdoor scenes, including car chases in what was supposed to be an 'inaction' film. World wide, the picture took in $45 million, which meant after TV and cable sales, the little film with the big movie stars would turn a modest profit. Even if the critics overall were not charmed, the public response – as evidenced by the box-office – must have encouraged Stallone.

*Cop Land* didn't do *Rocky* or *Rambo* business; and the reviews didn't glow, but then the critics rarely praised a Stallone performance or film. None of these discouraging elements discouraged movie studios and independent producers, who continued to send their wish lists to Stallone's office.

Disney proffered *Enemy of the State*, a conspiracy-fuelled action drama with Stallone cast as a liberal lawyer targeted for assassination by a secret US government agency. Blockbuster behemoths, *Beverly Hills Cop II* director Tony Scott and producer Jerry Bruckheimer, were attached. Stallone, however, became detached when he read the script. Of all his projects, this one was closest to going into production when the trades announced it was being put on indefinite hold pending re-writes.

Also placed even further on the backburner was *Into Thin Air*, a thriller to be produced by Steven Spielberg protégé Brian Grazer (*Apollo 13*). Maybe Stallone had second thoughts because the director was Lili Zanuck, better known as a Hollywood wife (Mrs Richard Zanuck) than for her directing début, the flop *Rush*.

Less likely, the trades announced that Stallone would star in the sequel to *Men in Black*. Reports noted that neither of the original stars, Will Smith or Tommy Lee Jones, was contractually obligated to do the sequel. The implication was that the film was Stallone's for the taking. So far, he hasn't taken.

Helpful Miramax, hopeful that Stallone found the *Cop Land* experience a joy (except for the binge and diet parts) and would stay on board, bought the rights to the *Rambo* series from the bankrupt owner, Carolco, for the firesale price of only half a million dollars.

An iffier project, *Rules of Engagement*, has director William Friedkin (*The French Connection*) on board, but Stallone will only say that he is 'in talks' about the drama which mixes *Platoon*-like battle scenes with a courtroom drama *à la A Few Good Men*.

Tellingly, Stallone has turned down the man who briefly revived his career in 1993 with *Cliffhanger*, director Renny Harlin, and an offer of $12 million to star in an action sci-fi movie, *Frequency*. Harlin is a notorious micro-manager, like the star. Plus, Stallone's unhappy forays into science fiction fantasy, *Judge Dredd* and *Demolition Man*, may have scared him away from the genre.

The writer-director-actor has said he is happiest when he's alone in his office with the door closed, writing. In fact, the superstar is also a superwriter in terms of box-office. A survey of screenwriters from 1985 to 1995 ranked Stallone at number five, with his scripts grossing half a billion dollars during that decade alone.

While he chooses his next acting project, the screenwriter keeps flicking his Bic. He's written *Rocky VI*, based on the life of over-the-hill champ George Foreman, but he doesn't plan to make the film, describing the process as 'therapy' rather than a viable project. 'Not to make. Just for fun. Like a diary,' he said.

The actor loves writing so much, he has even stooped to cable, very *déclassé* for a movie star. But it's for a cause close to his heart. A huge financial contribution from the actor recently bailed out the struggling inner-city church headed by Rev Vincent Spann of the Faith, Hope and Deliverance Ministry in Miami. Stallone is writing a cable script based on Spann's life and work.

Of all his writing projects, the most intriguing also contains the mostly unlikely subject matter considering his past interests and preoccupations. Stallone 'confided' at a press conference held by the Hollywood Foreign Press Association last August that he is writing an historical epic about the Turkish massacre of Armenians during World War I. A month before the press gathering, Stallone was coy with a reporter from *US* magazine, saying only, 'I'm writing a screenplay on a historical event from 1915, which I have to really remain quiet about. It's an epic. I don't know if I'm right to star in it. It could do the film a disservice. So I might go with an unknown.' The *US* reporter had no clue about *the* most important event of 1915, the Armenian holocaust, and dimly asked the star about the project, 'Does stuff blow up?'

Stallone said, 'Yes. But it blows up *with class*.' Could the epic be his *Schindler's List*?

For some reason, the star was more forthcoming a month later with the foreign press, maybe because foreigners have always given his films a better reception. Stallone identified the subject as the Turkish government's genocidal policy towards Armenians during the war and compared the situation to 'Masada', in which Jewish rebels committed suicide *en masse* rather than surrender to a Roman army in the first century AD. Then, in a sublime example of how unaware he remains about his clout, Stallone added this caveat: 'I don't know if [the project] is ever going to happen.' No doubt, after Miramax's Weinstein and every other mogul in Hollywood found out about the revelation at the foreign press gathering, these powerbrokers grabbed for the phone, begging Stallone to let the epic 'happen' with them.

But first, he'd have to reload the Uzi for another film with even more 'stuff' blowing up when Miramax announced plans for a fourth apparition of John Rambo.

# Chapter Seventeen

# A Rocky Love Life

Six years after his break with Brigitte Nielsen, Stallone still felt bitter about romance. In 1993, he condemned the very concept of love: 'It takes intelligent persons and makes them walk around with their thumb in their mouth, becoming human drool cups. It takes people who run entire nations and turns them into babbling idiots.'

Nielsen may have been the first woman to step out on him, but she wasn't the last. Stallone's romantic relationships in the '90s had as many ups and downs as his film career. Nielsen had burned him badly and publicly. His heart seemed protected by asbestos as he dated so many models and starlets a national magazine felt it had to keep a month-by-month tally of Miss January, February, etc.

'After my second marriage failed, I didn't want to be rejected again, to be broken-hearted and left. For a while, I didn't believe that real, lasting affection existed.'

Stallone wasn't too badly burned and found his lovelife seriously re-ignited only a year after the split with Nielsen. *People* magazine listed Jennifer Flavin, a then 19-year-old model from the San Fernando Valley, as 'Miss September' in a 1988 photo spread of the superstar's dates. Eventually, Flavin would become 'Mrs January through December' and Mrs Sylvester Stallone, but the process would take a decade and involve several embarrassing, public infidelities on her future husband's part.

For all his cynicism after the Nielsen fiasco, Stallone remained a romantic, even a naïve one who still believed in love at first sight. If he could fall in love with a photo of Nielsen slipped under his hotel-room door, it isn't hard to imagine his falling big time when he saw another gorgeous model *in person*, Flavin. 'The first time I saw her, I knew I had found what I was looking for. This is someone you could look at and know you love her more than you did a second before,' he said.

A mutual friend had introduced them at a West Hollywood restaurant in 1988. Besides stunning looks, Flavin was smart. A part-time model who didn't seem particularly career-driven, she was a full-time student, majoring in psychology at Cal State Northridge in suburban Los Angeles. Stallone had several beautiful women, starlets, models, wannabe whatevers, at his table. When he asked what Flavin did for a living and she told him she was a college student, the other women, whose aspirations didn't extend beyond becoming a movie star or marrying one, laughed in Flavin's face.

It wasn't Flavin's unusual career goal that caught Stallone's attention. And certainly not her singular beauty, since he was constantly surrounded by the stuff. It was her failure to be intimidated or impressed by him. 'I wasn't like, "Oh, my God, it's Stallone!" I didn't care to be on the arm of a famous man,' she said.

Two days later, Stallone called and asked her to go horseback-riding. Pretty soon, they were a couple. But for the first five years of the relationship, the twosome kept separate establishments. He had the Malibu pad and Pacific Palisades palazzo. Flavin lived with her mother in the San Fernando Valley until 1991, then moved into a modest, two-bedroom condo in a less ritzy suburb south of Los Angeles, Manhattan Beach.

Although they didn't live together, Stallone made up for in generosity what he failed to provide in proximity.

A Cartier watch, a Mercedes, living-room furniture for her mother – these were some of the gifts he bestowed on his off-screen leading lady.

Flavin, despite her early independent stance and refusal to

be intimidated, soon found herself worshipping at the altar of this muscular deity. 1988's self-possessed psychology major seemed to have turned into a Stepford Girlfriend by 1993. On the set of *Demolition Man*, a reporter called Flavin a 'proper dream of girlie perfection'.

Perfection worshipped perfection. Flavin described the ideal man, and he turned out to be *her* man. 'I just watch and I listen and he fascinates me. He just intrigues me by what he does and says. He may talk a certain way to you or to someone on the street, but when we get home, the way he speaks to me – so eloquently . . . And he writes poetry and he paints and he can direct and he can and he can . . . everything. There are just so many things about him . . . He's funnier than any comedian I've ever met. He's so smart. He writes, he sings, he paints. I consider him a Renaissance man.'

While the statuesque Flavin, at five feet nine and 120 pounds, had become a successful model by 1993, it was Stallone's body that got the praise. 'Flawless' was the way she described his gym-perfected physique. While he slept, she would perform an *ad hoc* body-fat test without calipers. The test results, according to her, showed zero per cent body-fat. 'I look for fat when he's sleeping at night, and I can't squeeze any. And he's got a perfect behind. It's like a little peach,' she said.

Her fellow-perfectionist, however, found flaws in her body, and didn't hesitate to point them out. When they woke up, Stallone would begin the day with a visual inspection of his bed partner. She said: 'In the morning, he tells me what's wrong with my body.'

Once, he threw a tantrum about her diet, but she attributed the it to the pressure of writing a script, not as a personal attack. Flavin was in bed, eating jelly beans. Stallone had earlier told her to lay off candy, and when he found her disobeying, 'He started screaming at me for eating them. He broke a plate and threw the Gummy Bears [jelly beans] at me.'

Less than a year later, the relationship had ended. Flavin's 'Dear Jennifer' letter from Stallone combined modern technology with old-fashioned heartlessness. He dismissed her via Federal Express. 'He sent me a six-page handwritten letter, in pen. It was pretty sloppy,' she said.

The letter listed a number of reasons why he was bailing, but not the most important one. Her modelling agent, who was better connected, told her the truth. Stallone was involved with a retired model turned photographer, Janice Dickinson, who had given birth to a baby girl two weeks before Stallone dumped Flavin via overnight delivery. Dickinson's baby was Stallone's, the new mother announced.

Flavin had no idea about this other woman, much less the new baby. 'It hit me like a ton of bricks,' she said. Based on earlier comments by both parties, however, it sounded as though Flavin knew the score, she just ignored it. In 1991, Stallone practically announced monogamy was not one of his family values. 'When we come together, it is wonderful. When we are separate, there are no strings attached. That's the way it is. No strings.'

Marriage, he stated more bluntly, was not on his 'to do' list either. 'She's a wonderful girl,' he said about Flavin in 1991. 'But I like her too much to marry her. She doesn't deserve that kind of anguish. Actually, I want to be romantic forever. I want to be cryogenically frozen with a box of chocolates under my arm and some flowers, and thaw me out in 200 years so I can propose to someone. In other words, I don't want to lose it,' he said, without specifying what he feared losing. Certainly not Flavin, who remained devoted, although 'co-dependent' is the term other observers used.

Flavin seemed to accept the stringless commitment in 1992. 'I'm not naïve about what may go on when I'm not around – he's a 45-year-old man – I can't change the way he is. Still, he's not a cheating dog *every* day of the week. We spend five out of seven nights together, so I don't know where he'd find the time.' A year later, Flavin apparently felt they had decided on monogamy. At least, *she* had. 'We date exclusively,' she said in 1993, and discredited rumours that her boyfriend was not a one-woman man. 'We wouldn't have a relationship otherwise,' she insisted. And if her lover did stray? 'I would leave, definitely.'

Before she could leave, however, Stallone left her. In

retrospect, Flavin conceded her rose-coloured glasses were more like opaque when accepting her boyfriend's claims of monogamy. 'I'd always hear things,' she said in 1994 shortly after Federal Express arrived with the bad news. 'But he'd always kind of defuse the situation. He'd say, "Oh, she just wanted a picture with me" or something like that. Being a star, people are always going to talk about you.'

She missed other signs that she didn't have his undivided attention. When he flew to the Miami set of *The Specialist*, he told Flavin to stay behind. She attributed the cancellation to first-day shooting jitters. The real reason Stallone told his girlfriend to stay put: the mother of his daughter, Dickinson, and their baby, had arrived in Miami.

'I thought he was just a little nervous about moving to Miami and starting a new movie. Now I know he was a *lot* nervous,' she said, giggling. 'But his nervousness had nothing to do with pre-production problems.'

Flavin refused to feel sorry for herself. And she hadn't completely devoted herself to her man. Although she cried when she got the six-page farewell letter, career obligations kept her mind off the split. The former college student and Stallone worshipper had forged an independent career for herself in the four years they had been together. *People* magazine called her 'one of fashion's hot models', signing contracts with Revlon and other major accounts and earning $5,000 a day on the catwalk. In her spare time, she was looking for a new fella. '[I'm] dating. I'm working it, babe,' she said.

If revenge, as the Spanish proverb goes, is a dish best served cold, Flavin may have been gratified that her ex-lover was soon eating chilled crow.

As Stallone's new consort, complete with an heiress to the throne, Dickinson became a celebrity, if not in her own right, at least in her boyfriend's reflected light. At 39, her modelling career long over, Dickinson found herself a star all over again, meriting a major interview in *W*, the fashion trade magazine. She knew the source of her fame and self-deprecatingly admitted it. Photographers didn't besiege her and magazines didn't beg for interviews to discuss her career as a photographer.

Dickinson conceded, 'No one writes about my modelling or photography . . . All they really have to say about me is that I'm the mother of Sylvester Stallone's child.'

This is where the crow tartare comes in. Dickinson's little girl, Savannah Rodin Stallone, had been misnamed. DNA tests, which were somehow leaked to the press, showed that baby Savannah needed to change her last name. Stallone was not the father.

Nielsen's alleged philandering had been embarrassing for the superstar stud, but at least Brigitte had denied having extramarital affairs. Baby Savannah's DNA test publicly proved he had been cuckolded by his new love.

A 1994 interview with the star only hints at the rage he felt about yet another public humiliation. 'After the DNA test I went my own way, and I see [Dickinson] saying terrible things, like, "In the eyes of heaven, it's his!"' Stallone implied that Dickinson had been seeking child support, which she denied. 'Well, have the church pay your rent!' he said about her alleged request for money. 'Have the Pope pay your car rental!'

He wasn't alone – or out of love – for long. In 1995, Stallone announced his engagement to yet another supermodel, Angie Everhart, then 25. Like Nielsen, Stallone had fallen in love with a picture before he fell for the real thing. A photo of Everhart on the cover of *In Fashion* magazine prompted him to call her, but not for a date. The helpful star just wanted to introduce her to a movie producer he felt could jumpstart her acting career.

Friends brought them together a few weeks later at the House of Blues, a trendy nightclub on the Sunset Strip in Los Angeles. Stallone had been dating another model, Andrea Wieser, a 22-year-old from Austria. We don't know if the Austrian beauty received a Fed Ex letter, but soon Everhart and Stallone were more than an item. They were *fiancés*. In April 1995, they announced their engagement in a press release. 'We are very much in love,' their joint statement crowed, 'and we couldn't be happier.'

Tentative plans to marry in the Vatican's Sistine Chapel were dismissed as a joke by the couple. Then Everhart was dismissed. The whirlwind courtship ended as a tempest in a tabloid. The mainstream press remained mum on the reason for the break up, and this time Stallone kept his feelings to himself. Or at least, didn't share them with national magazines.

Less than a month after the announcement of his engagement to Everhart, the marriage was not only off, but Stallone had returned to the long-suffering Flavin.

In the closest he ever came to an apology, he described his decade-long on-again-off-again relationship with the model in Job-like terms. And Flavin was Job. 'There was a period where I was going through a complete period of irresponsibility.

'Jenn proved that she really loved me . . . having lived through everything . . . Her ability to forgive,' he added, was 'almost of Biblical proportions . . .'

In August 1996, they had a baby girl, Sophia. The child was born with a serious heart defect, which was corrected by surgery ten weeks after birth. Doctors repaired a hole in the infant's heart. 'This child . . . for the first time I really understand what it's like to look into an infant's eyes and know you would die for this person. At the hospital I said if I get through this, this child will never learn to walk, because I'm never going to put her down.

'Now for the first time, I know this is it. I'm not going anywhere. It won't get any better. And it's going to work.'

Although he wasn't going anywhere, the twice-burned star wasn't rushing to the altar. It took him almost a year after his daughter's birth to commit to a third marriage. The star and the model were married on 17 May 1997 at the Dorchester Hotel, followed by a lavish wedding reception at Blenheim Palace, home of the Duke of Marlborough. Not the Sistine Chapel and wedding cake with the Pope, but Blenheim was not exactly Cold Duck at Motel Six either.

Sadly, a second daughter, due December 1997, was lost when Flavin miscarried in July of that year. Stallone consoled his wife, saying, 'That's OK, we'll try again.' Indeed, almost exactly a year later, on 27 June 1998, the couple had another daughter, named Sistine, at an undisclosed hospital in Los Angeles. The baby girl's name may have been an ironic references to her parents' whimsical plan to marry in the Sistine Chapel.

Stallone remains content if somewhat confused about the source of his contentment. 'I'm happy. I can't define it.'

His brother-in-law, Mitch Flavin, gave it a shot. 'When they got back together, it seemed they knew what they wanted. She knows that Sly is pretty much settled down. He's getting older too, you know,' Flavin's protective older brother said.

Stallone seemed to have Rambo's take on romance. Not only war, but love is hell too. 'I've been given many opportunities, and I've failed many times, and I've learned from it and used it. It's a process. Only through failure did I appreciate success. I may have lost many battles, but I still enjoyed . . . the war.'